Cultivating a Life for God

By Neil Cole

St. Charles, IL 60174
1-800-253-4276

Published by ChurchSmart Resources

We are an evangelical Christian publisher committed to producing
excellent products at affordable prices to help church leaders accomplish
effective ministry in the areas of Church planting, Church growth, Church
renewal and Leadership development.

For a free catalog of our resources call 1-800-253-4276.

Cover design by: Julie Becker
Manuscript edited by: Kimberly Miller, Robert Rummel and Rachel Wetzler

ISBN 1-889638-06-4

Table of Contents

Acknowledgments

First, I want to acknowledge all those who were my companions in growing and multiplying as disciples: Kenny Peterson, David Sincock, Doug Bukowski, Pam and Steve Strunk, Dan Koning, Ken Allen, Don Burghardt, Dennis Muoio, Chuck Conway, Joe Ayer, Kevin Fairchild, Mike Bivens, Chris Wright and Kelley Kildall. Each of you helped me to grow closer to my Lord and was also used by Him to teach me all that is in this book. You are my joy and crown! Stand firm beloved.

Bob Logan, Phil Helfer and Chris Suitt have been of immense help in strategic thinking. Your influence is found on many pages of this book and in my life as well.

Some of my friends around the world who have encouraged me and tested the transferability of these concepts in other cultures deserve recognition for their contribution. Steve Addison and Colin Noyes in Australia, Paul Klawitter and Florent Varak in France, Tim Berends in Canada, Paul Kaak and Ed Waken in the US, and Dave Guiles in Argentina have each helped to refine my thinking and tested the profound simplicity of these principles.

Finally I wish to acknowledge my wife and best friend on earth, Dana, for her always-practical voice of wisdom. The fact that you know me so well, Dana, and still believe in me is a constant source of support. Thank you.

Dedication

This book is dedicated to those pioneers who are willing to blaze new trails for the sake of the gospel rather than a salary, and who will make and multiply disciples to raise a church for the harvest from the harvest. You are the real heroes of our generation. May God multiply your numbers in the days ahead!

Biographical Information

Neil Cole is executive director for Church Multiplication Associates, a church planting ministry for the Grace Brethren Churches, Southwest USA. He is also a church planter himself in the greater Long Beach area of Southern California. He co-authored *Raising Leaders for the Harvest* with Robert E. Logan.

Foreword

The book you're now holding can revolutionize your ministry! *Cultivating a Life for God* provides a biblical process for making disciples that results in godly character, evangelistic fruitfulness, and multiplication. What you find here is not simply theory — the principles have been proven effective in ministry situations. I like the Life Transformation Group process because it is:

1. **Focused** on the task of making and multiplying disciples. Too many Christians, even pastors, lose sight of the prime directive that our Lord Jesus Christ gave to us just before he returned to heaven. Believers who focus on loving obedience to Jesus not only become better disciples, but make more disciples who also reproduce.

2. **Balanced** on being, knowing, and doing. Believers who allow the Word of God to permeate and saturate their lives grow in their knowledge of God and biblical understanding. Confession of sin encourages personal holiness and cultivation of Christlike character. As the lives of growing disciples are transformed, they reach out to those who have not yet experienced the transforming power of Christ.

3. **Flexible** and adaptable. Since the Life Transformation Group process is rooted in basic biblical principles, it can be applied very easily within any cultural context.

4. **Reproducible**. Lengthy training sessions are not necessary to implement Life Transformation Groups. The process is very transferrable so that even new believers can effectively make and multiply disciples.

I have been familiar with Neil's ministry for a number of years. He is a man of integrity who has a passion for raising up leaders from the harvest. While focusing on reaching people for Christ, he exhibits an equal commitment to increasing the spiritual depth of disciples and empowering them to realize their full potential. Neil integrates careful biblical and theological reflection into a fruitful and expanding ministry that brings glory to God.

No matter where you labor in the harvest and the church, you will find practical guidance for establishing a reproducing process of making disciples. May you use this book to significantly advance the kingdom of God.

Bob Logan
CoachNet International

Chapter 1:
Lesson in Lifesaving:
Remember the Prime Directive

Jesus was a busy man. His things-to-do list was extensive. Matthew 9:35 describes the kind of busy life He led. It says, "And Jesus was going about *all* the cities and the villages, teaching in their synagogues, and proclaiming the gospel of the kingdom, and healing *every* kind of disease and *every* kind of sickness (emphasis mine)."

Jesus, in spite of his busy calendar, never failed to keep in mind His prime directive—*to seek and to save those who are lost* (Luke 19:10). In the midst of His busyness, He took the time to lift up His eyes and see the multitudes. The Bible goes on to say, "And seeing the multitudes, He felt compassion for them, because they were distressed and downcast like sheep without a shepherd."

When I get busy, I tend to forget the most important reason why I'm here, my prime directive—*to make more and better disciples* (Matt. 28:18-20)! In fact, unlike Jesus, the busier I become, the more I lose compassion for the lost. It doesn't take much for the multitudes to become more of a stumbling block to impede my effectiveness rather than a reason for becoming effective. Freeway traffic is a cause of frustration rather than compassion. A busy parking lot gives me a headache from the confusion rather than a heart that aches with compassion. A long line is an obstacle rather than an opportunity.

Compassion is not a common virtue today. It is hard to imagine how we can be surrounded by lost and drowning souls and not care, but it's true. Perhaps because we see so much violence and death on the TV each night we have become hardened to hurting people. Perhaps the reality of their suffering doesn't sink in. Perhaps we justify our inaction, thinking it is not our responsibility to care for the needs of lost people. Perhaps we leave it to people more gifted, more trained, more professional ... more compassionate.

Chuck Swindoll tells the story of an actual court case in the state of Massachusetts back in the late 1920s:

> It concerned a man who had been walking along a pier when suddenly he tripped over a rope and fell into the cold, deep waters of that ocean bay. He came up sputtering, screaming for help, then sank beneath the surface. For some reason he was unable to swim or stay afloat. His friends heard his faint cries in the distance, but they were too far away to rescue him. But within only a few yards was a young man lounging on a deck chair, sunbathing. Not only could the sunbather hear the drowning man plead, "Help, I can't swim," he was also an excellent swimmer.
>
> But the tragedy is that he did nothing. He only turned his head to watch indifferently as the man finally sank and drowned.
>
> The family of the victim was so upset by that display of extreme indifference, that they sued the sunbather. The result? They lost the case. With a measure of reluctance the court ruled that the man on the dock had no legal responsibility whatsoever to try to save the drowning man's life.[1]

Swindoll goes on to say, "You and I have a legal right to mind our own business—to turn a deaf ear to anyone in need, to continue sunbathing while someone is drowning. We are not obligated to respond. Indifference may not be illegal, but it is certainly immoral!"[2]

The truth is, compassion cannot be something pushed on us from obligation, it is something that comes out from within. In fact, the word "compassion" used of Jesus in this passage literally means "bowels"—it is something you feel in your gut. Compassion, real compassion, doesn't come about by lawsuits. It is a natural feeling that stirs in your stomach and comes out in your eyes, your words, and your actions. It takes "guts" to care for the lost!

I can't accept that if we love Jesus we will be able to sit back and sunbathe while millions all around us drown. I believe that the reason we don't feel compassion is that we don't really see that the multitudes are indeed drowning.

We all need to regain the compassion that Jesus felt in His gut when He took the time to see the multitude. There are times when I intentionally go to a crowded shopping mall or a busy restaurant and just stand among the throngs asking the Lord to break my heart. It may take a while, but the Holy Spirit begins to open my eyes to the lost people who are distressed and downcast. They are shepherdless sheep. They aren't just heading to the next department store but to a Christless eternity.

It was in this context that Jesus identified the one thing lacking for us to see a great harvest of souls (Matt. 9:37). He also told us where we should go to find what we need. But first take a moment to notice what He didn't say. He didn't say, "The harvest is plentiful, but the dollars are few." Nor did Jesus say, "The harvest is plentiful but the property is too expensive." He didn't say, "The harvest is plentiful but we first need the latest self-help book or practical program."

No, the missing ingredient isn't pennies, property, parking lots or programs. Jesus said, "The harvest is plentiful but the workers are few." He is clear when He says that it is "workers" who are missing. With workers we can bring in a harvest.

Where do we go to find workers? Bible colleges and seminaries? Parachurch ministries? Harvard School of Business? Churches? No, none of these answers are right according to this passage. The place where we need to go to find workers for the harvest is on our knees before the throne of God. Jesus said, "Therefore beseech the Lord of the harvest to send out workers into His harvest (Matt. 9:38)." The harvest begins with prayer to the "Lord of the harvest."

Jesus not only identifies what we're missing, and where to find them, but He also provides for us a great example of how to raise up workers for the harvest. He called them out of the harvest itself, empowered them and sent them right back into the harvest as workers doing the very same things He himself had modeled. Jesus multiplied His ministry.

In this passage of Scripture, Matthew, the author of this gospel, is a great example. In the ninth verse of this chapter Jesus calls Matthew to follow Him leaving behind tax audits, accounting books and piles of money. In verses 37-38, he has Matthew praying for workers to go out into the harvest and then two verses later Jesus is sending Matthew out into the cities and villages (Matt. 10:1) to do what He himself had modeled in ministry (Matt. 9:35). He goes from tax collector to preacher in the course of one chapter of scripture. Most would think that this is too soon to send Matthew out into the harvest fields. He's too new, too easily influenced, he doesn't have enough knowledge to answer people's challenges. But Jesus saw Matthew as having many contacts with other lost people who need the gospel (Matt. 9:10-11). He also saw Matthew's new life change as a very persuasive presentation of the gospel in itself. He may not have had depth of knowledge but he had a passion for Christ that many who have been Christians for years lack. I'll take a hot, impassioned witness over a cold, knowledgeable one every time. We can grow in our knowledge, but getting the passion back is not as easy. People don't respond to cold facts, they are moved by passionate people who have a testimony of the difference Christ has made.

Jesus shows us that the workers must come from the harvest itself. He transforms the twelve from being disciples ("students" or "pupils") in chapter ten verse one to being apostles ("sent ones") in verse two. They went from praying for the harvest to preaching in the harvest in one verse.

We can draw from the flow of this passage a simple chain of action that can be a road map for an abundant harvest:

If we can't *see* them, we won't *love* them (Matt. 9:36).

If we can't *love* them, we won't *pray* for them (Matt. 9:36-38).

If we can't *pray* for them, we won't *win* them (Matt. 10:1).

If we can't *win* them, we won't *send* them (Matt. 10:2-5).

What is needed for a harvest? Prayer and workers. The more prayer we offer, the more workers we will see. The more workers raised up, the greater the harvest. This is a simple solution that Jesus gave us because He wants more than anything to be a shepherd for the lost sheep who are distressed and downcast.

The only barrier we face to a greater harvest is a lack of compassion that motivates prayer, which releases workers, which yields the harvest.

James says, "You have not because you ask not" (James 4:2). My friend Bob Logan has said, "You ask not because you care not."[3] I would add, "You care not because you see not." We need to see what's going on. Jesus said, "Lift up your eyes and look on the fields that they are ripe for harvest (John 4:35)."

For seven years I worked as a lifeguard on the beaches of Los Angeles. I spent most of my days working on the world famous Venice Beach, so I have many stories to tell. Of all the rescues that I made, one stands out in my heart as the most meaningful. I believe that it can teach us something about the importance of seeing the harvest with compassion in the midst of our busy lives.

One day each week I worked what is usually a slow tower called "Ave 23" in Venice Beach. The tower is tall and sits up high on the berm above a rock jetty. The real reason for the tower's placement is to be a bridge of vision and coverage. The tower was manned mostly to provide backup for the guards at either of the two towers beside it because their vision was blocked by the high berm and jetty. Consequently, those who work this tower usually get to watch the action more than participate in it.

On the north side of the jetty is a popular surfing spot. On the south side is a popular stretch of beach good for sunbathing and swimming. This beach has a steep berm and the waves tended to be mostly shore break (where the waves crash right on the beach). The only real danger at this beach, besides skin cancer, is what we called "gutter rips". A riptide is a current that pulls out to sea just past the swells of the waves (commonly misnamed "undertow"). A gutter rip is where shore break crashes up on the sand berm, gathers together in one place and then is pulled back out to sea for the next wave. Usually they are pretty harmless and can be fun for kids to play in. Occasionally, when the surf is strong they can be dangerous for small children and need to be monitored closely.

Another reason that this tower exists is to keep people from climbing on the rock jetty, which can be dangerous. On this particular day the surf was big and the people were enjoying it. I was sitting down, comfortable, in my high tower, listening to music and watching life happen. I noticed some kids, local surfers, climbing out on the jetty to get a good view of the waves. I remember thinking to myself, "They're alright, they know the conditions and probably won't get hurt. They climb up those same rocks every day after the lifeguard goes off duty. They won't get hurt." I was about to let them go, but my conscience kicked in and wouldn't let me go.

Wrestling with myself I remember finally deciding, "This is what I'm supposed to do, it's what I'm paid to do." Finally, I got up out of my comfortable chair, turned off the music, put on my jacket, put on my sunglasses, grabbed my rescue can (a red flotation device that has a rope attached which you can strap around your shoulders to pull people to safety), slid down the ladder, walked down the berm to the water's edge and called out to the young people (who were pretending not to hear me).

As I was waiting for a response I did something which is natural and instinctive for all lifeguards—something we have been trained and ingrained to always do. I glanced around looking at the water in my area. No matter what else we may be called upon to do, watching the water is never an option for lifeguards, but always a prime directive of utmost importance. This is what lifeguards must do. It is why we are there. It is so important that we are programmed to do so by constant reinforcement, training and education until it finally becomes habitual. The lifeguard has a prime directive—watch the water and save lives. That simple. Everything else must come second.

I remember that day, looking south over my shoulder, seeing the area and turning back to finish yelling at the kids on the rocks when what I saw suddenly registered in my mind with a jolt of adrenaline. I saw, about 150 feet away, ten little fingers and the top of a small head poking out of the water rapidly flowing out to the large crashing surf in a gutter rip. A mother was quickly running after them.

This is the kind of moment that defines a lifeguard. It is the culmination of all his or her training and working. He or she can never truly anticipate a moment like this, but must be ready for it at any time, for it can come without warning. It can last only a few seconds and is never more than a few minutes. As quickly as it comes, it is done. To not be ready is lethal. It is why lifeguards exist.

I immediately took off sprinting down the beach. I tossed off my sunglasses. I tore my jacket off and threw it down in the sand. I unwound my rescue can and put it on over my shoulder. By the time I reached the place where I originally saw the child and mother I couldn't see either. The Pacific Ocean spread out before me was all I saw.

Instinctively I dove into the water in roughly the place where I last saw the child. The odds of rescuing someone after they have submerged in the ocean are very small. When you factor in the vastness of the ocean, the smallness of a child, the poor visibility of the water and the ocean currents and waves you begin to see how hopeless a rescue is once a child has submerged. A "needle in a haystack" doesn't even begin to describe the challenge. Unfortunately, a beach that has shore break usually means that the water gets deep immediately.

Time is of the essence for obvious reasons. In most, three minutes is when brain damage occurs for lack of oxygen. But in the ocean another fatal danger exists. If someone aspirates salt water the eventual damage to the lungs is ordinarily lethal. Some live through the ordeal, only to drown days later in lungs full of infection. As I dove under the water with my arms and fingers stretched out wide, trying to rescue this child by braille, intuitively I uttered a prayer that I would somehow find him in time. "Oh God, help me find this kid!"

Jackpot! I felt flesh. It was the torso of a small boy, a baby—my hands could almost encircle his whole rib cage. Instantly, without seeing anything, I planted my feet and shot my hands up through the surface of the water lifting the boy up into the air to breathe. After he had gasped and breathed in a lung full of oxygen I rose to the surface myself to get air. I immediately began walking up to the beach, holding the boy in my arms. He still hadn't begun to cry because he was trying to hold on to every molecule of air he could consume. As I marched up the sand, another gutter rip started fighting against us. Just then I felt the strap around my neck tug hard against me. I looked back and found mom holding on tightly to the rescue can on the other end of the rope. I managed to drag the three of us up to the warm sand.

I put my ear to the boy's back to listen for any gurgling from aspirated seawater and heard nothing but clean lungs. Of course, by now, everyone on the beach could hear those lungs—a most welcomed sound!

This boy is alive today because I was busy doing the things that lifeguards are supposed to be doing. I was down on the wet sand, close enough to reach the boy before it was too late. If I had been up in the tower, I am confident that I wouldn't have made it in time. But being busy down on the beach wasn't enough. I would have never seen the boy if I had not remembered my prime directive and scanned to see if there was anyone in the water who needed to be rescued.

Life can keep us busy, but it is there in the midst of our busyness that we need to open our eyes and see if there is anyone in desperate need of a Savior. The moment we have been called upon to save a drowning soul can come in the midst of our busyness and we need to be prepared. Jesus was a busy man, but He never lost sight of His prime directive—to seek and to save those who are lost.

Every one of us can bring the Savior to drowning men, women and children who are distressed and sinking fast. But we first have to see them and care. Our purpose here on earth goes beyond basking in the goodness of the Son. We can no longer afford to turn a deaf ear to those who are drowning all around us.

I was not the first lifeguard in my family. In fact, I am a third generation ocean lifeguard in southern California. My grandfather, father and uncles all watched the same beaches that I did but with one dramatic difference—

I made many more rescues. There were some times when I would make more rescues in a single day than they did in a whole summer. My father used to be amazed at that fact, even a little skeptical. I used to say that it was due to the increase in the population in our area, all the while knowing the real reason—my dad and his brother can't see! They are both extremely nearsighted. They were outstanding watermen; in fact, my Uncle, Peter Cole, is a legendary big wave surfer in Hawaii where he still surfs even in his late sixties. But it doesn't matter how good your lifeguarding skills are if you can't see those who are drowning!

You may wonder how in the world these men could be hired by the city of Los Angeles to watch the beaches when their vision is so bad. There is an explanation, but it only makes matters worse. They had a surfing buddy named Buzzy who was in excellent physical condition. Buzzy couldn't swim very well but he also wanted to lifeguard. They worked together to pass the qualifying exams. Buzzy would show up to take their eye test in the physical exam while my father would show up and take the swim test under Buzzy's name. What's worse than a lifeguard who can't see? One who can't swim. You may wonder who would take the swim test for my father—his identical twin brother, Peter, would take the test twice, once for himself and then return later under the alias of his brother.

In case you're wondering, the testing process is far more scrutinizing now. Yes, it's safe to go back in the water.

This comical tragedy points out a crying need in the church today. We obviously need believers who can see those who are lost and drowning, but we also need to be able to rescue them. It isn't enough to be capable in disciple-making if we remain blind to those who need it. It also doesn't help to see the harvest if we don't have the ability to make disciples of them. I contend that we are not doing well at either.

It is my hope that this book will help you to be able to see those who are drowning, but also know how to reach out and offer them salvation in such a way that they in turn can reach out and do the same for others.

In this book, I will first examine some foundational principles for multiplying disciples. I will then share the background behind the discovery of a system that incorporates the principles for multiplication. I will then explain a simple system called Life Transformation Groups. This system can release spontaneous growth and multiplication in your church. Finally, I will examine the advantages as well as the most common objections and questions people have about the system.

While this book does contain a very practical means to release multiplication of disciples, it is not just a "how-to" book of discipleship methodology. You will find that the first half of this resource is principles. In fact, the methodology given in this book is so simple that it would only take a little over a page to communicate (which is part of the genius of the strategy). But the principles that are shared in these pages are the heart and soul of effective multiplication of disciples and should be understood. I have found that the implementation of the model without a grasp of the principles will often lead to frustration and failure. Granted, most of us like to receive practical "how-to" methods that can be immediately applied and effective, but the truth is that without the framework of the principles and values described in this book, the methodology lacks a healthy environment in which to thrive.

Hear me when I say that it is not the methodology that transforms lives, it is only the power of the gospel of Jesus Christ applied to a needy soul by the Holy Spirit. The methodology is only helpful in that it brings the desperate sinner into prolonged contact with God and His word in the context of community with others who are also pursuing the Lord.

Chapter 2:
The Need for Life
Transforming Power

The church of Jesus Christ in the Western world is at war, but from all external appearances, seems to be losing! The United States was born as a nation seeking a free expression of faith in Jesus Christ. For many years, we were the leading people in taking the gospel around the world, fueling revivals in foreign lands with missionary enterprises. Today, we see mostly the residue of the faith of a previous generation. Whereas once we were the missionary nation, today we have become a mission field in desperate need of the gospel.

Currently the US is the fifth largest unchurched nation in the world with over 187 million Americans who remain untouched by the gospel.[4] Of the adults who do attend any given protestant church on a typical Sunday morning, half are not even Christians.[5] Churches lose 2,765,000 people each year and between 3500 and 4000 churches close their doors each year for the last time; while only 1100-1500 churches are started.[6] Not a single county in all America has a greater percentage of churched people today than a decade ago.[7]

Tom Clegg, co-author of *Releasing Your Church's Potential*, asks the question, "If this is a Christian nation, why is it that the largest church in the world is in Seoul, Korea, while the largest Buddhist temple is in Boulder, CO.? If this is a Christian nation why is the second largest church in the world in Nigeria, while the largest Muslim training center is in New York?"[8]

Somewhere in our past we became institutionalized and our church life became busy and complicated with buildings, budgets, buses and bureaucracy. Not that we shouldn't be busy, but we have somehow lost sight of the prime directive given to us by Jesus Himself: To "go and make disciples of all the nations." More of the same isn't going to make the difference. We need a miracle.

There is hope. We can still fulfill the great commission in this generation, but we will need to get back the power that spread the gospel across the globe in the first century. We will need to see multiplication of disciples occur among all those in the church. We must deploy all the troops in a charge against the gates of hell.

The Awesome Power of a Transformed Life

The miracle we need most right now is one that the Lord has freely given us already. It is the power of a changed life. The world is poised and ready to see the relevance and power of our message if only we would let them see it firsthand.

An episode of the television show "ER" demonstrates the potential power that the church has. It was an episode in which Dr. Mark Greene (played by Anthony Edwards) is in a particularly cynical mood and challenges nurse Carol Hathaway (played by Juliana Margulies) to see if there are as many sane patients as kooks who come through the emergency room. Dr. Greene, believing that the number of kooks far out-distances the number of sane patients, wins the contest. I will do my best to portray this episode accurately from my memory.

In the midst of the episode, black Physician Assistant Jeanie Boulet (played by Gloria Reuben) uncovers an unconscious patient's torso to reveal a Ku Klux Klan tattoo over his heart. She asks Dr. Greene to find someone else to care for this patient but he declines. Later, the patient regains consciousness and is actually a very gentle and polite man. When Boulet enters his room, cold and indifferent, to give him sutures, she asks him to lower his gown and at first he is reticent and asks for a different nurse. She insists and he lowers his gown revealing the tattoo. He then asks her a most profound question. He asks, "Do you believe in the power of God to change a life?" She retorts, "What does that tattoo have to do with God?" He said, "Well, I was hoping you wouldn't have to see that tattoo, that's why I requested another nurse. It's not something I'm proud of. But the Lord Jesus Christ has changed my life. Whereas once there was nothing but hatred and fear in me God has now changed me and I have love and faith. Let me ask you again, do you believe in the power of God to change a life?" In a fashion uncharacteristic of Hollywood, ER set the testimony of a life changed by the gospel of Jesus Christ as the only sane one in the midst of wackos and crazy people (including some of the doctors themselves).

A little later in the episode, Boulet is still contemplating the question she has been asked. She probably recalled all the people she had known to find any who have indeed changed. She is so struck by this man's testimony that she even asks it of an associate, "Do you believe that people can change?" This is such a great example of the potential power we have available to us. Most people believe that people can change, but when they take the time to truly consider their own friends and acquaintences they will be hard pressed to find a single one. The power of the gospel will stand out boldly today against a backdrop of people living out their lives without any true power.

There is no power on earth more potent than the gospel in a heart of belief (Romans 1:16). Ed Silvoso puts it like this, in his book *That None Should Perish*, "The church has been entrusted with something that every politician on earth would give an arm and a leg to have: the power to see hearts changed." We have been given this power, though we generally leave it unused. Our pews are full of "Christians" whose lives show little difference from those who are in the world.

We already saw in Chapter 1 that Jesus valued the power of a changed life when He called Matthew and immediately put him into service. The New Testament has many examples of people who have only just met Jesus, have little knowledge of His person or work and yet are already able to effectively stand up to others with a bold witness. They do so all on the irrefutable persuasion of a changed life. My favorite such story is found in the ninth chapter of the gospel of John.

One Saturday, Jesus and His disciples were walking through Jerusalem and happened to come across a man born blind. The disciples asked Jesus a question, "Who sinned, this man (in the womb is implied) or his parents?" Of course the greater question is, "Is it fair that God should have this man suffer all his life for the sins of his parents, or worse, for some sin he could commit in vitro?" But Jesus answered the question with something remarkable. In essence He said it wasn't for sin that he was born blind but for this very moment. Then He did the strangest thing. (All Bibles should carry a warning label at this portion of Scripture that reads: "Warning, do not try this at home.") He spat on the ground, scooped up the muddy saliva and smeared it on the eyes of this unsuspecting man. He then gave this stranger a verbal command and said, "Go, wash in the pool of Siloam." Which he did.

This man did not ask to be healed or saved. Jesus took the initiative and did so in a rather unorthodox if not rude manner. He didn't even introduce Himself. What's worse, spitting in someone's eyes or throwing dirt in someone's eyes? The correct answer is "all of the above." Later, after the miracle of seeing, the man described what Jesus did in more sanctified terms,

"The man who is called Jesus made *clay*, and *anointed* my eyes, and said 'Go to Siloam and wash (emphasis mine).'" We do tend to soften Jesus' actions and words, as though He needs our protection. I am convinced that Jesus wasn't shy about making a lasting impression on people who otherwise would've lived the rest of their lives in mundane routine. To "diplomatically" dilute His actions and words, no matter what the motivation, leads to a mere characterization of the real God-man and is tantamount to idolatry. He doesn't need our suggestions.

The man obeyed Jesus, which demonstrates at least some measure of faith. Of course, who wouldn't want to wash his face with saliva and mud spread on your eyes? He was healed as a result of this small amount of faith.

This Sabbath miracle created quite a stir among the town. Everyone was questioning if this was indeed the man born blind. He just kept on saying with glee, "I am the one." He wanted to tell the world what Jesus had done for him. He wasn't shy about it. This was the best thing that ever happened to him and he wanted to tell everyone. The people would give him his day in court. They took him to the Pharisees.

It is here in the legal proceeding that we watch as the seeing man becomes just that—a man who sees. Watch as his emerging faith and conviction grows in the heat of examination and debate.

The Pharisees began an inquiry into this event because, in their eyes, a law was broken—the Sabbath law. They were not the slightest bit amazed by the miracle standing right in front of them, all they could see was that their petty rules had been broken. The Jewish leaders by this time had laid down some 39 extra rules to limit people from doing most anything on the Sabbath day.[10] All were punishable by stoning.

A debate ensued among the Pharisees over whether a sinner could perform such miracles or not. In the midst of this discussion the Pharisees made a mistake; they asked the seeing man what he thought of this Jesus. His answer came without hesitation—"He is a prophet."

The Jewish leaders couldn't accept this conclusion so they began a ridiculous pursuit—to refute that this man was indeed born blind. They wouldn't accept the evidence in front of them so they called in testimony of other eyewitnesses; they called his parents to the stand. Fearing the decree that had already gone out—that if any would confess Jesus as the Christ he or she would be excommunicated from the synagogue—the parents simply identified him as their son and validated that he was indeed born blind. As to how he could see, they did not venture to answer but referred to their son who was old enough to speak for himself. That got the Pharisees nowhere. Back to square one.

Getting frustrated by a lack of progress the religious leaders turned again to the seeing man and said, "Give glory to God; we know that this man is a sinner." It is interesting that Jesus declared in the beginning of this whole story that this man was born to give glory to God by demonstrating His miraculous work in him. He was, in fact, fulfilling the Pharisees' very request when he acknowledged the miracle Jesus had done.

While the Pharisees were appealing for him to give the credit to God and not to this "sinner" named Jesus, the seeing man declared an irrefutable argument in behalf of his new emerging faith. He said, "Whether He is a sinner, I do not know; one thing I do know, that once I was blind, now I see." There is no answer for this from the Pharisees. They can spout theology and pious statements of condemnation, but they can't challenge this simple statement of faith coming from a man who knows next to nothing about Jesus. He may not be an expert about the law, theology or the identity of the Messiah, but one thing he is qualified to be an expert on is his own experience. No one can challenge this.

Out of frustration they asked the seeing man once more how Jesus performed the miracle. By now, the man was weary of this whole proceeding and he began to see that these religious men don't have any answer to his statement. This gave him a growing sense of confidence. These men were not so "untouchable." When they asked how it happened again he began to exert some of his strength and a bit of good old-fashioned sarcasm. He said, "I told you already, and you did not listen; why do you want to hear it again? You do not want to become one of His disciples too, do you?"

Confronted with this strong, uneducated witness who couldn't even read, the Pharisees began to feel threatened and react with their usual condemnation and pious recital of religious credentials for being right. They pronounced what they considered to be a grave accusation meant to hurt him, but in reality was the greatest compliment the seeing man had ever received. They said, "You are His disciple, but we are disciples of Moses." Then they went on to spout some theology and said, "We know that God has spoken to Moses; but as for this man, we do not know where He is from."

I think it was at this point that the seeing man felt a great release. He had never thought of himself as a disciple of anyone. Until this moment he was an outcast, a loser. Now he was a disciple of Jesus! I don't think he even thought of such a possibility until his highly tuned ears heard it for the first time from his accusers. He didn't even know Jesus yet, but suddenly he is a disciple of this man whom everyone talks of. He felt a little bolder, a little more confident of his position. The Pharisees had fallen unsuspecting into a trap when they said in essence, our master (Moses) is better than yours (Jesus).

With this new boldness that came from identifying with Jesus, the man took the initiative. He went on the offense in front of the untouchable Pharisees! Without waiting to be asked he said, "Well, here is an amazing thing, that you do not know where He is from, and yet He opened my eyes (the Pharisees never like it when they're told that they don't know something). We know that God does not hear sinners; but if anyone is God-fearing, and does His will, He hears him. Since the beginning of time no one has opened the eyes of a person born blind. If this man were not from God, He could do nothing."

The seeing man was beginning to see even clearer. He suddenly began to understand that Jesus was greater than these hypocritical Jewish leaders. They played the "my-master-is-better-than-your-master" game by comparing Jesus with Moses, and now the seeing man began to expound on something of which he was an expert—the healing of people born blind. Not even Moses was able to do that! No one, since the beginning of time, had been able to do that! Checkmate.

This offended the Pharisees who had no argument except to once again resort to condemnation and to propound the superiority of their own position in life. They brought the story back full circle to the original question (one which the now seeing man probably heard), "Who sinned, this man or his parents?" They said, "You were born entirely in sins, and are you teaching us?" And with that the blind men excommunicated the seeing man.

Even this last attempt at criticizing and condemning the seeing man was a backhanded compliment. Just think of it. Only a few hours earlier he was a poor blind man with no hope and no respect, begging on the streets for some food. All who saw him assumed him to be a wretched sinner, otherwise God wouldn't have made him blind. Now, after a brief encounter with this mysterious man named Jesus he was standing before the great and educated Pharisees, and as they admit he was teaching them! He was teaching them theology! His teaching was not only sound, but his argument in the end won the debate. Their attempt to label him as one born entirely in sins only encouraged him more because Jesus had already proven, irrefutably so, that he was not born blind because of his sins. He could see! There was no evidence that he was born entirely in his sins as was once thought, at least not anymore than anyone else. No, the ones who evidenced bondage to sin and blindness were his opponents, not this man.

A question begs to be asked from this unusual event. Why did Jesus choose to perform this miracle in such a strange way? Jesus told us why in the very beginning. He said this man was born blind "in order that the works of God might be displayed in him." Jesus healed him in a delayed fashion so that the seeing man could be brought before the Pharisees alone and Jesus would not be the one defending His own actions. I believe Jesus wanted the man to stand before the Pharisees, having never even seen Jesus and knowing little of Him, to refute and totally embarrass them. In the course of their debate, he was able to identify Jesus as a prophet, having come from God and performing miracles that no man has done in all of human history, superior even to Moses. Jesus had already done so, but when an uneducated, formerly blind beggar and notorious sinner does so then God gets even greater glory for the miracle of a changed life.

A fascinating fact is that just a short time earlier Jesus had been in debate with these same Pharisees and they accused Him by saying, "You are bearing witness of Yourself; Your witness is not true (John 8:13)." Jesus responded in two ways. He first said, "Even if I do witness of Myself, My witness is true; for I know where I have come from, and where I am going; but you do not know where I come from, or where I am going."

The second thing He did was to send this witness to defend where He came from. And he defended Him admirably. We often think that we need to send our most knowledgeable and intelligent people to witness to this world. We think that it is our education and philosophical arguments that will convince people of Jesus. The truth is that the most persuasive and effective argument for the validity of Jesus' claims is the testimony of a changed life. This powerful ammunition is given to any and all who follow Him. It doesn't require a high IQ, a degree or high position in life. Any one of us, no, every one of us has this power available.

We also tend to think that if some famous and successful person becomes a Christian he or she will be a more effective witness. There is a theological word to describe this point of view—"hogwash". The kingdom has much to offer all that come to Christ, and it isn't needing anything from the world.

The fact is that the most destitute and broken people who are changed by Jesus become the greatest witnesses of God's power. Remember the Samaritan woman at the well (John 4:28-30; 39-42)? What about the Gerasene demoniac set free and commissioned to stay behind (Mark 5:1-20)?

Do you find it amazing that Matthew is a despised tax collector at one moment (Matt. 9:9), hosting an evangelistic outreach party the next (vv. 10-13), and then sent into the cities as an Apostle to preach the gospel just a few verses later (Matt. 10:2 ff.)?

Look again at these people God chose to use. A promiscuous Samaritan woman? A notorious and naked, demon-possessed, super freak? A poor blind beggar respected by none and assumed to be a sinner by all? A hated traitor tax collector? Each was selected and empowered by Jesus Himself. In our world of fabulous celebrities and over-qualified experts we are not accustomed to selecting ignorant and disrespected common people to lead our outreach efforts. Jesus did. In fact, almost as alarming are the prospects He discards. A wealthy young man, a leader among his peers, and who was considered of the utmost integrity was outright turned away by Jesus (Luke 18:18-25).

Is this because knowledge, training and maturity are not needed? No, of course not, in fact, this was Jesus' training and maturing process which begins (and ends) with a bold witness of Christ. But one thing this does show us is that a person who has nothing but Jesus is enough to win others to Christ.

Perhaps we have lost faith in the power of the gospel to truly change and empower a life. Perhaps we have more faith in our programatic church training systems than in the gospel itself. I do know one thing is true, we believe that the darkness of the world is more powerful to destroy God's life than the light of a new life is to invade and overcome that darkness. I believe this is evident by the separatist and protectionist position we take over any that do come to faith. I believe that our well intentioned protection is not truly protecting the child of God but rather the lost souls who would be changed drastically if allowed to encounter the real Christ.

I hope that the church can raise the level of her faith in the power of the gospel and lower the level of qualifications needed to be a servant of Jesus in this world.

Even seemingly successful people need to come to understand their own brokenness and desperate need for Christ before they are of use in the kingdom.

Charles Colson was among the most powerful consortium in the world when he advised President Nixon. Later in life, in a moment of reflection while speaking at a prison event, he realized that it is at his point of greatest weakness that Jesus used him most. He writes:

> As I sat on the platform, waiting my turn at the pulpit, my mind began to drift back in time ... to scholarships and honors earned, cases argued and won, great decisions made from lofty government offices. My life had been the perfect success story, the great American dream fulfilled. But all at once I realized that it was not my success God had used to enable me to help those in this prison, or in hundreds of others just like it. My life of success was not what made this morning glorious—all my achievements meant nothing in God's economy. No, the real legacy of my life was my biggest failure—that I was an ex-convict. My greatest humiliation—being sent to prison—was the beginning of God's greatest use of my life; He chose the one experience in which I could not glory for His glory.
>
> Confronted with this staggering truth, I dicovered in those few moments in the prison chapel that my world was turned upside down. I understood with a jolt that I had been looking at life backward. But now I could see: only when I lost everything I thought made Chuck Colson a great guy had I found the true self God intended me to be and the true purpose of my life."[11]

Colson goes on to say, "It is not what we do that matters, but what a sovereign God chooses to do through us. God doesn't want our success; He wants us. He docsn't demand our achievements; He demands our obedience. The kingdom of God is a kingdom of paradox, where through the ugly defeat of a cross, a holy God is utterly glorified. Victory comes through defeat; healing through brokenness; finding self through losing self."[12]

The man Jesus personally selected to be His witness before these accusatory Pharisees who had challenged His authenticity was anything but predictable! He chose the most lost and forgotten man He could find and sent him before the wolves to declare His glory.

After this "seeing man" had done battle and defeated the Pharisees, Jesus came to him and asked, "Do you believe in the Son of Man?" This was the first time he had ever seen Jesus with his eyes, but he recognized His voice. This extraordinary witness then said, "And who is He, Lord, that I may believe?" He still didn't know much, but he did know his Shepherd's voice (John 10:27). He had been called a "disciple of Jesus" by the Pharisees and was excommunicated for it. Now he identified himself as a disciple by referring to Him as "Lord". His once simple and small faith had blossomed into a bold witness and a gentle surrender to his Lord.

Jesus responded, "You have both seen Him, and He is the one talking with you." This is a profound statement. Jesus intentionally separates the experience of having "seen Him" (past tense) with "talking with you" (present tense). I believe that He was referring to more than just his ability to see Jesus with his eyes, but to his really seeing whom Jesus was, which occurred sometime earlier in front of the Pharisees. Jesus was talking about enlightenment, not just vision, although it sure is amazing that this man born blind could now see Him.

The seeing man responded in faith and said, "Lord, I believe." Then the gospel says he worshipped Him. Who needs a synagogue when you've got Jesus right in front of you (John 4:21-24)! After being exposed to the weak and corrupt hypocrites who were in charge of the synagogue, I don't think it was difficult at all to adjust to being with Jesus as an outcast of the religious system of the day. This was a system in which he was already an outcast simply because of his disability. Finally, he was somebody with meaning that could contribute and even defend the Messiah before rulers! Jesus not only repaired his vision, He gave the seeing man hope and significance. His life now had meaning and purpose because of Jesus. He was completely healed and changed forever.

Jesus puts a capstone on this miracle of seeing by saying, "For judgement I came into this world, that those who do not see may see; and those who see may become blind." His commentary on the debate was that his witness was the winner, hands down—in more ways than one.

This true story exemplifies the awesome power of a life that has been touched by Jesus. Such a life is immediately empowered to be a change agent in this world. The church has traditionally hid these precious converts from the world in an attempt to protect them. Jesus shows us that it is the world that needs the protection from these powerful change agents. When we hide them from the world we sever the contacts they have with other lost souls who are, in fact, the very best evangelistic fields since they get to see the power of Christ demonstrated in this converted life firsthand. We also communicate to the world that we are defensive and we hide the very power we have that will set them on the defense. Why would the world want to believe our message if we feel the need to protect and keep its results safe from exposure to the world? Let me tell you that the world won't believe our message until we do!

There is also another detriment to hiding our new converts from the world—their own faith is stunted. We think that we are helping them by separating them from the wolves, but this is not what Jesus did. He said, "I send you out as sheep in the midst of wolves (Matt. 10:16)." In examining this story we were able to see the emergence of a sincere and powerful faith in the seeing man as he dialogued and defended Christ before the Pharisees. There is no better way to learn theology than in dialoguing with those who don't believe. They will challenge you to think out what it is you truly believe. In the process it will be your own faith, not that of your pastors, parents or professors.

In the book, *Dedication and Leadership*, written by Douglas Hyde who was once a top trainer of communists before he converted to Catholicism, he explains that the best way to solidify new converts to communism was to set them out alone on a street corner handing out communist propaganda. When opponents attacked them they found themselves fighting for their convictions which did much to cement them in their soul, just as it did with the seeing man in this story.

Perhaps this is why every young Mormon must spend a year going door-to-door talking with people about the merits of Mormonism. I firmly believe that by trying to protect our young converts we have done more to deprive them of growth than to help them to grow.

We need an army raised up of men, women and children who can say, "One thing I know for sure, where as once I was blind, now I can see." "Once I was an alcoholic and now I am free." "Once I was an angry, hateful man in the KKK and now I love." "Once I was a prostitute and now I am pure." "Once I was homosexual and now I am free to live righteously." This will be our most persuasive argument for the reality and veracity of the gospel. Any argument without this will fall on deaf ears.

This is the power that the church is meant to display. It's not our rational arguments, grandiose buildings, elaborate television broadcasts or bold personalities that will win this world to Christ. It is our simple testimony of a life that has been forever changed by the power of Christ who has come from heaven to seek and save those who are lost that will leave the world speechless.

This is where we need to start if we want to change the way things are. It begins with a single life that is transformed and who can then say to others, "Here is an amazing thing, that you don't know where He is from, and yet

He opened my eyes." It begins with one, but with this kind of power it can soon spread to others.

Addition of new witnesses is a part of the Lord's plan, but alone it is not enough. We must begin to think in terms of multiplying these new believers who have a passionate testimony.

The Awesome Power of Multiplication

In his book, *Disciples Are Made Not Born*, Walter Henrichsen described a display at the Museum of Science and Industry in Chicago which featured a checkerboard with 1 grain of rice on the first square, 2 on the second, 4 on the third, then 8, 16, 32, 64, 128 etc. Somewhere down the board, there was so much rice that it was spilling over into neighboring squares—so the display ended there. Above the demonstration was a question: At this rate of doubling each square, how much rice would you have on the checkerboard by the time you reached the 64th square? To find the answer to this riddle, you punched a button on the console in front of you, and the answer flashed on a screen above the board: Enough to cover the entire subcontinent of India, 50 feet deep![13] There would be 153 billion tons of rice—more than the world rice harvest for the next 1000 years.[14]

Henrichsen concludes:

> The reason that the church of Jesus Christ finds it so hard to stay on top of the great commission is that the population of the world is multiplying while the church is merely adding. Addition can never keep pace with multiplication.[15]

You may have heard the fable of a father who offered his two sons a choice of either one dollar a week for 52 weeks, or one cent the first week, and then the amount doubled the next week to just 2 cents and, continuing for 52 weeks. One son took the buck; the other took a chance and accepted the penny. We all know who wins: the son who took the dollar would have 52 dollars at the end of the year. The one who began with a penny would have by the end of the year, enough money to pay off the national debt, and still have plenty left over for himself![16] That's a father with some deep pockets!

Multiplication begins slower than addition, but like a car rolling down a steep hill, it builds in momentum as it goes. What starts with a penny and then two cents later becomes millions, and then billions and within a short time trillions.

To illustrate this, Christian Schwarz and Christoph Schalk, in their *Implementation Guide to Natural Church Development*, give the following example:

> Imagine a water lily growing on a pond with a surface of 14,000 square feet. The leaf of this species of water lily has a surface of 15.5 square inches. At the beginning of the year the water lily has exactly one leaf. After one week there are two leaves. A week later, four. After sixteen weeks half of the water surface is covered with leaves.[17]

The authors then ask, "How long will it take until the second half of the pond will also be covered? Another sixteen weeks? No. It will take just a single week and the pond will be completely covered."[18]

Multiplication may be costly, and in the initial stages slower than addition, but in the long run, it is the only way to fulfill the Great Commission in our generation.

We Cannot Cause the Growth, Only Release It

How can we cause spontaneous growth and multiplication of changed lives? We can't. Jesus made it clear in a parable given to His disciples that we don't cause the growth, we merely introduce the elements that can release the growth. He said,

> The kingdom of God is like a man who casts seed upon the soil and goes to bed at night and gets up by day, and the seed sprouts up and grows—how, he himself does not know. The soil produces crops by itself, first the blade, then the head, then the mature grain in the head. But when the crop permits, he immediately puts in the sickle, because the harvest has come (Mark 4:26-29).

Jesus tells us that the farmer doesn't know what causes the growth. Today, in our more technologically advanced society with powerful microscopes and chemical engineers we still don't know what causes the growth. We know what is needed to allow the growth—but then so did the first century farmer. We can describe the life force, we can release it, but we can't create it. We can explain how the process works down to the tiniest particles, but we are still like the farmer in the parable—we don't actually know what causes it. We do know, however, how to plant seeds, water them and watch.

In spite of our complex ignorance, the Bible has simple answers. In the parable mentioned above, Jesus teaches that if the right elements are in place, the crop grows "by itself." Paul wrote in 1 Cor. 3:6-7, "I planted, Apollos watered, but it was God who caused the growth. So then neither the one who plants nor the one who waters is anything, but God who causes the growth." As the Psalmist says, "He (the Lord) causes the grass to grow for the cattle, and vegetation for the labor of man (Ps. 104:14)."

The real question we need to answer is "How can I release a spontaneous multiplication of growing disciples in my community?" The answer lies in planting seed in the soil. Fruitfulness begins with the good seed in good soil. God created all living things to grow and reproduce. We already have all that we need to see this happen in the church, we need only release the natural elements God designed and placed in all His living things.

In the sixth chapter of the gospel of John, Jesus tested His disciples with a challenge to do the impossible. He told them to feed a crowd of well over 5000 hungry people in a lonely place close to the Sea of Galilee. Having had only 200 denarii (a denarius was worth about a day's wages) they turned to Jesus in futility without any hope of fulfilling His desire. In a mustard seed amount of faith, Andrew volunteered another's lunch. He said, "There is a lad here who has five barley loaves and two fish, but what are these for so many people?" Andrew could see the multitude, comprised of about 5000 men and probably many more women and children, and offered the school boy's sack lunch with a sigh of resignation. "What are these for so many people?" The fact that he even mentioned the boy's lunch reveals the smallest amount of faith. With this, Jesus took the five flat barley cakes and two fish, prayed, and then broke them up and distributed them to the multitude. In Jesus' hands the food was multiplied and fed all to their fullest with twelve baskets full of leftovers.

The masses of lost people in the world are so many. The church in the West, such as she is, is not much. We need to turn to Jesus with what little faith we have and say, "Here is something, not much, not enough, but something." Unless we are in Jesus' hands we cannot possibly reach the hungry souls of the world.

In my office hangs a picture that is not only a beautiful piece of art, but a constant challenge to me. It is a drawing by the late Richard Oden, former head of the illustration department of the school of fine arts at California State University of Long Beach. The drawing is of two fish and five small loaves. The loaves are composed in such a way that they resemble a person on his knees lifting his arms to the Lord. Handwritten under the drawing it says, "'There is a lad here with five barley loaves and two fish, but what are these for so many?' For Neil and Dana from Dick Oden, June 4, 1983."

While I was studying art at CSULB under Dick's mentoring, I accepted Christ as my Savior and then a couple years later, received my call to ministry and chose not to pursue a career in the arts. Though Dick was not a Christian he seemed to understand what my life was becoming and with perception often lost with preachers he somehow discerned that this one verse would summarize my life. He drew this picture and gave it to Dana and me at our wedding.

Dick saw that I was a boy with little to offer the Lord to feed the multitudes, but in the hands of Jesus I was enough. When Jesus chooses to multiply our lives He can reach the whole world, but it begins with a mustard seed of faith and the surrender of all we do have.

I believe that Jesus is still testing His disciples. I believe He wants us to look at the task at hand with what little resources we have and turn to Him and say, "It's not much, but here, take my life." Unless we are given into the hands of Christ we are nothing more than a humble sack lunch, but in His hands we can see multiplication fill the hearts of the multitudes.

Chapter 3:
Principles for
Passing the Baton

Someone has said, "Last words are lasting words." The words we share with loved ones in the last moments of our lives are usually most important in nature. If you knew that you had just a few days left to live how would you spend your time? Would you watch television? Read a novel? Lay out in the sun to get a tan? Go shopping at the neighborhood mall? I doubt it. You would probably spend that time with those most important to you. And you probably wouldn't talk about the weather and how the local baseball team is doing in the playoffs. Most of us would make sure that our words were memorable and significant, because they would be our last.

I once had a close friend who was dying of cancer. I went to visit with him during his last days. He was at home. As I entered the room the first thing I noticed was the smell of death which seemed to be anxiously waiting in the room like a vulture hovering over some hopeless animal. There were machines with small lights flashing and an occasional beep. These machines were for the expressed purpose of managing the pain Jim was enduring from the invasion, which had now consumed much of his body. I was at a loss for words and said little of anything, which was probably the best thing for me to say. I was there to minister to Jim, but in an amazing way Jim ministered to me. After we spoke for a time I was getting ready to leave. Jim said to me, "Neil, I have something very important to tell you, but I can't tell you now, I'll have to tell you tomorrow." I said I would come by the next morning. That night he died. I have wondered ever since what he wanted to tell me. One day he'll be able to tell me, but I believe that it will not be so important at that reunion.

Fortunately for all of us, we are not left wondering what the apostle Paul's last words would be. Second Timothy is Paul's last will and testament. Written in his final hours while in a dungeon on death row, Paul passed on his most pressing words to his apprentice and successor. As you would imagine, this is a very personal and passionate letter. At a time when one would look back over his life, Paul asks himself, "What will survive of my influence in this world?" In his letter, he charges Timothy with the responsibility to carry on the great work after he is gone. Here, in Second Timothy, we find the principles Paul wants passed on in the discipleship relationship. He shows us what ingredients are essential if we are to see lives changed and ministry multiplied and if we're to have an influence down through the generations that follow us.

Paul starts the second chapter by explaining the importance of multiplying disciples and leaders for the strength and future of the church. He says, "You my son, be strong in the grace that is in Christ Jesus, and the things you have heard from me in the presence of many witnesses, these entrust to faithful men who will be able to teach others also."

There are three initial observations I want to make from this passage. They are what makes a strong and growing church, and what motivates and facilitates this kind of multiplication. We will then discover in the following chapters what sort of people make the best candidates to begin such a process and what are the most essential disciplines that need to be present for a life to be transformed. We will then propose an explanation of the best context in which to see these principles applied so that life transformation and multiplication is released. Finally, we will conclude this section with an illustration of how God began a movement of life transformation and disciple multiplication in an otherwise normal looking church.

1. The Strengthening of the Church: Strong disciples make a strong church, growing disciples make a growing church.

The first principle for leaving a lasting legacy of multiplication is that it all begins with being a strong disciple yourself. It doesn't start with what you do but with who you are in Christ. E. M. Bounds once wrote, "Men are looking for better methods, God is looking for better men."[19]

Christ does not want to multiply weak and feeble Christians; such would only make matters worse. He wants to multiply strong disciples. This is why Paul starts by admonishing Timothy to first, "be strong in the grace that is in Christ Jesus." It is in Christ's grace that we are strengthened to be fruitful disciples. It is also grace that we give to others when we make and multiply disciples. Grace is given to us to give to others. The more His grace has transformed our own lives, the more it will touch the lives of others around us As I once heard Chuck Colson say, "You cannot export what you do not have."

A strong church begins with a strong disciple who makes more strong disciples, who then go on to make more, and so on and so on and so on. This has always been the Lord's intention for His church. Paul tells us that a strong Christian is a reproducing Christian. A strong church, likewise, is a reproducing church.

Strength comes in multiplication. In fact, multiplication is an awesome power. It is the principle of multiplication that releases the explosion in an atomic bomb. It was the multiplication of disciples which eventually allowed a handful of disciples to become a thriving church that outlived and overcame the most dominant World Empire of all history—the Roman Empire. Today, we are a part of the church because the Christians of every previous generation took the Great Commission seriously and passed the faith on to others.

This is what makes the church vital and strong. This is also what makes the church last. The Great Commission is for all Christians, not just those who are professional Christian leaders. When we take the Great Commission out of the hands of every Christian, we immediately weaken the whole church and diminish her longevity. When we set the Christians to fulfilling the Great Commission, the church immediately and ultimately is healthier, more vital and enduring. As Rick Warren, pastor of Saddleback Community Church in southern Orange County, California, has said, a church's strength is not determined by her seating capacity but by her sending capacity.[20]

2. The Stimulus of Real Growth:
The carrot works better than the crop.

The second principle for multiplying significance has to do with our motivation. We've all heard the expression, "You can lead a horse to water, but you can't make him drink." There are varieties of ways to motivate a horse: spurs, a bridle, a crop and of course the proverbial "carrot on a stick." The crop and the carrot will both motivate a horse. A crop is a little whip used to slap the horse on the rear and motivate it to run. When you want the horse to pick up the pace you simply spank him with the crop. That would probably work with people as well, but I don't suggest you try it. A crop will only work as long as a rider is there to apply the pressure, while a carrot will motivate a horse any time he sees one. If a horse walks into his stable and sees a crop hanging on the wall he does not immediately break into a canter. But, if a horse enters his stall and sees a carrot lying on the floor in the corner he will go get it. One form of motivation applies external pressure, while the other taps the horse's internal desires. While it is true that you can't make a horse drink, you can salt his oats, which will make him thirsty and want to drink the water.

The motivation for following Christ and reproducing disciples must be internal rather than external. Paul appealed to Timothy with passion because he would soon be gone. Timothy would no longer have Paul to challenge him. If the drive for making disciples doesn't come from within, the process will eventually break down and will not carry on. Disciple-making that truly reproduces is propelled by an intrinsic motivation.

Proverbs 16:26 says, "A worker's appetite works for him, for his hunger urges him on." I don't usually have to motivate myself to eat. Hunger does that for me. Most of us do not need external motivation to eat though we may need it to not eat. The food industry thrives because we all have an internal drive to eat. There is another industry which does well but which exists to help motivate us to not eat—the diet industry. You would think that the two are in competition but in reality, the diet business does best when the food industry does well. The food industry taps our internal motivation and is far more successful than the diet industry, which utilizes external motivations.

Paul appeals to the internal motivations that will keep Timothy going even in the face of hardship and setbacks. He uses several analogies and admonitions to demonstrate the drive we need to have that will see us through even in the face of suffering hardship. There are six key motivational factors that Paul appeals to in this brief passage. He cites three natural incentives and then three spiritual incentives for the Christian life. They are as follows:

Natural Motivations:

1. A desire to bring pride to those whom you are responsible to. Paul writes: "No soldier in active service entangles himself in the affairs of everyday life, so that he may please the one who enlisted him as a soldier (2:3-4)."

2. A desire to be the best we can be. Paul describes this motivation when he says, "If anyone competes as an athlete, he does not win the prize unless he competes according to the rules (2:5; 4:6-8)."

3. A desire to benefit from the results of our efforts. Paul says, "The hard-working farmer ought to be the first to receive his share of the crops (2:6)."

Spiritual Motivations:

4. Moved by the love of Christ demonstrated in His sacrifice for our sins. Paul charges, "Remember Jesus Christ, risen from the dead, descendant of David, according to my gospel, for which I suffer hardship even to imprisonment as a criminal; but the word of God is not imprisoned (2:8-9)."

5. A compassion for the lost and dying souls in this world, who are headed to hell without Christ. Paul describes his own motivation with these words, "For this reason I endure all things for the sake of those who are chosen, that they also may obtain the salvation which is in Christ Jesus and with it eternal glory (2:10)."

6. Inspiration rooted in the character of God. Paul reminds us, in poetic fashion, of God's faithful character. He says, "It is a trustworthy statement: For if we died with Him, we shall also live with Him; If we endure, we shall also reign with Him; If we deny Him, He also will deny us; If we are faithless, He remains faithful; for He cannot deny Himself (2:11-13)."

All of these motivational incentives are internal drives that will cause someone to delay immediate gratification in order to aspire to a greater cause. Paul urges Timothy to remind the church of these things (2 Tim. 2:14). These are the motivations that create a hunger for Christ and a drive to stay the course in the face of opposition (2 Tim. 2:3, 9).

The key to effective disciple making and multiplying is to tap internal motivation. Many discipleship methods, however, resort to external motivation, which is much weaker. We have people sign a "contract" (or we spiritualize it and call it a "covenant") stating that they will fulfill the obligations of the method. Or, as many encourage today, we keep an empty chair in the meeting to remind us to reach out to others. If empty chairs ever did win people to Christ, most of our churches would be experiencing revival. How many of us really share the gospel so that a chair will be filled? Far better that our motive be to have heaven filled. Pardon my expression, but I really mean it when I say—to hell with the empty chairs!

I once had a boss who would fine us $1 for every minute we were late to a staff meeting. Once we resort to this kind of tactic we have already lost the battle. If the meetings were such that the staff felt better for having been there, the leader would not have to resort to such manipulation to get the meetings started on time. By adding the fine, he actually made the meetings less attractive. If one were a few minutes late it was better to find an excuse not to go at all.

If the disciples don't want to move forward, but do so only out of guilt and obligation, then as soon as the pressure is removed the process will end. Even while the external compulsion is present, the process will lack quality because the disciples will lack enthusiasm.

The basis of Christianity is the new covenant, in which God writes His law, not on tablets of stone, but on human hearts (2 Cor. 3:1-11). The reason that Christianity continues is not because we have better rules than other religions, or stiffer punishments for breaking the rules. The reason that the church continues generation after generation is because God changes hearts by regeneration. Christianity begins in a heart that is set on fire from heaven and cannot be quenched on earth. Any incentive less than that will ultimately hurt the cause rather than help it. The good news of salvation by grace through the death and resurrection of Jesus is the spark that will change a heart and provide incentive for obedience the rest of our lives.

If the Spirit of God doesn't grip our hearts and move us to invest our lives in the most important cause of all then no manipulative tactics, gimmicks and persuasions will get the job done. In fact, this very idea is what separates true Christianity from all other forms of religion. It is the gospel that transforms a soul from within which is the essence of our faith. Everything we are and do should stem from this. The rest of the religious world appeals to external motivation and good works to merit a better life. If we appeal to the same then we offer nothing better than the rest of the false religions and cults available today. Christianity begins with the assumption that none of us can merit life and that we are absolutely dependent on help from above.

If you were given the choice of going into business with an all-volunteer staff or a paid staff, which would you choose? Most would opt for paid workers over volunteers. Why? Because it is easier to motivate them to do the job the way one wants it done. With financial remuneration, one can add bonuses, extra commission, a raise or other incentives. On the other hand, one can also threaten a loss of job or a drop in income if the work is less than desirable. External motivation does produce results.

If you were given a choice of going to battle against an all-volunteer army or an army of paid mercenaries which would you choose? I would choose the paid workers again. Why? Nobody in their right mind will take a bullet for a buck! Few men will risk their lives for the sake of a paycheck. That just wouldn't make sense. What kind of bonus is worth dying for? This is one reason why the Iraqi army rolled over so easily in Operation Desert Storm. They were on assignment motivated strictly by external influence rather than a cause. But an army of men who are willing to give their lives for a cause is hard to beat. The Soviet Union discovered this in Afghanistan. Superior weapons are often no match for hearts sold out to a cause worth dying for.

The church is an army of volunteers in a battle for the souls of people held captive. We must be willing to "suffer hardship as a good soldier of Christ Jesus." This is the kind of motivation that can turn a world upside down. We need to stop functioning as a business, concerned with the bottom line, and start acting like soldiers who are at war fighting for a cause worth dying for.

The kind of discipleship, which will make an impact on the next generation, will be the sort that grabs the heart of the disciple. Our methods must motivate from within and tap the disciple's intrinsic motivation rooted in a vital relationship with God (Rom. 2:28-29). Our discipleship must have no less a goal than a transformed life. Conformity to external behavior is not enough! We must set hearts aflame with passion for Christ. If we can't see our own lives changed by the power of the gospel, we have no right to expect to see the world changed by our message. If the gospel is not more important to us than life itself then the world will not be attracted to it. If they don't see us valuing the gospel why would we expect them to?

3. The Simplicity of the Process:
We must pass the baton with ease!

If disciple-making and multiplying is essential for all, we must find a way to make it available to all so that it can be passed on from generation to generation. Most methods have been far too complex and leader dependent to be passed on to others in such a way that they can then pass it on to succeeding generations. Not all Christians are meant to be leaders, but all are meant to be reproducing disciple-makers! The third principle for leaving a lasting legacy is to keep the pure message simple, and unencumbered by complex methodology.

Imagine if the relays at the Olympic track and field event required that each runner pass a lead baton instead of aluminum! The relays might still be entertaining to watch, but not for the right reasons. We watch the Olympics to witness athleticism, grace and skill, not slapstick comedy. I'm confident that the times would not drop but the baton would.

This is how our churches have approached discipleship in recent days. We most often fail to see multiplication occur because the baton we try to pass is too much. The disciple-making baton is so complicated and laden with unnecessary encumbrances that the work does not get passed on to the next runner, but rather is dropped. We must simplify the process so that it can easily be passed on without sacrificing the essential components that change lives.

As an art student in college, I learned a valued lesson which I have integrated into all I do. Less is more. The best things are simple things.

Three of the most feared words in a parent's vocabulary are, "some assembly required." Many have been up late at night on December 24th reading volumes of instructions in small type and three languages (none of which seems to be English) trying to put together a complicated toy for their kids. Ouch! The more complicated it is, the more that can go wrong with it. It is then that you can appreciate that "less is more."

We are often tempted to discount simple things believing them to be simplistic. A simple thing, however, can often be very profound. We dare not confuse muddy water with deep water. Just because a pool is muddy does not mean it is deep. Likewise, a crystal clear pool may appear shallow because the bottom is seen so easily, but may nevertheless be very deep. Simple is not simplistic.

In fact, I believe that simplicity is a step beyond complexity. What is easy is often simple, but simple is not easy. It takes great skill and effort to make something simple. It is easy to create something that is complex, you just keep adding "stuff" to it. To design something that is simple and yet profound, however, is a creative challenge.

Ralph Moore, founder of the Hope Chapel churches, which have multiplied into well over 100 churches worldwide, tells of an Eskimo tribe he read about which has only a 600 word vocabulary. He asked himself, "What would a translation of the Bible look like in that culture?" It would be pretty simple, straightforward and easily understood by all. Church must be reduced to the simple basics like that. God has intended for the most profound of truth to be able to be passed on—even in a language consisting of only 600 words. Of course, the task of the Bible translator is a challenge in that context. But God loves those Eskimos and wants to communicate His love and truth to them. He knew these people before the foundation of the earth and fully intended to translate His word into their language. It is possible, but also challenging. Ralph says, "I try to think of that Eskimo church when I make plans for my own church. How would our next ministry or program or sermon communicate in that church?"

Jesus said, "Come to Me, all who are weary and heavy-laden, and I will give you rest. Take My yoke upon you, and learn from Me, for I am gentle and humble in heart; and you shall find rest for your souls. For My yoke is easy, and My load is light (Matt. 11:28-30)." For most, discipleship has become so complicated that it is no longer an easy burden and a light load. But Jesus intends for the Christian life to be easy and light and to bring rest to our souls. Fulfillment of the Great Commission is meant to be restful, not stressful!

Simple is transferable, while complex breaks down. I remember one Christmas bringing home a large box for my then five-year-old daughter. The box contained an entire house—a playhouse made by a popular children's toy company. I remember opening the box with a degree of apprehension. The first thing I noticed was that there were no small parts, nuts or bolts, just the large heavy-duty plastic pieces that make up the playhouse. I then opened up the instructions that were surprisingly simple. They were simple diagrams without words of any language!

The first thing I looked for was a list of the tools that would be needed to construct this house, but there was none. This was a wonderful toy! I discovered that the house was put together much like a huge three-dimensional puzzle in which all the pieces snap together. Simple! That toy lasted years after my oldest daughter, her younger sister and their little brother's interest in it did. The colors faded some, but the house stayed strong, even though the children found it much more enjoyable to climb on its roof than to play inside. Eventually, we ended up selling it, completely intact and not weakened even a little. The designers who engineered that toy impressed me. They understood children and their parents and created something that is simple, enjoyable, and virtually indestructible.

When we approach disciple-making, wanting to pass the baton on to succeeding generations, we must refine the process so that it is simple and transferable. Simplicity is the key to the fulfillment of the Great Commission in this generation. If the process is complex, it will break down early in the transference to the next generation of disciples. The more complex the process, the greater the giftedness needed to keep it going. The simpler the process, the more available it is to the broader Christian populace.

The K.I.S.S. method works best for me. It stands for "Keep It Simple Stupid!"

Paul passed on to Timothy truths that were so profound that he would not forget them. They gripped his life and never left him. At the same time, however, the things Paul passed on were simple enough that Timothy could in turn pass them on to others who could then pass them on to others. The gospel itself is the most profound truth mankind has ever received, yet it is simple enough for a child to understand and pass on to others!

Perhaps the reason that we don't see multiplication of disciples more often is that we are trying to do too much too soon in the process. We fail to grasp the fact that discipleship, following Christ in simple obedience, is a life-long pursuit. We attempt to teach our disciples so much in the first year that we unintentionally sabotage the rest of the years by intimidating them into thinking it is way too hard for common people to do. We tend to overestimate what we can do in a year and underestimate what we can do in three years.

A helpful idea is for us to see disciple-making and multiplying as distinct from mentoring leadership. As was said above, all Christians are to be disciple-makers, but not all Christians are to be leaders. The word the New Testament uses for "disciple" means learner or pupil. A disciple is a follower of a leader, in this case—Jesus. The Great Commission is for all of us to make followers of Christ out of those who don't know Him.

By combining discipleship with leadership development we eliminate a good percentage of Christians from participation in the Great Commission. In reality, disciple-making is the foundation of good mentoring and leadership development. If we allow disciple-making to happen, unencumbered by complicated training methods, more will be able to do it and we will increase the pool to draw from for the purpose of mentoring leaders. Once we have growing and multiplying disciples we can build upon their emerging fruitfulness with intentional mentoring and training methods for those who demonstrate latent leadership potential.

We need to get back to the simple and yet profound basics when it comes to disciple making. When we attempt to teach all the theologies, disciplines and methods to a brand new Christian we slow down their obedience. The church is suffering from a bottleneck of teaching without obedience. In essence, we are educated beyond our obedience. Which is not to say that we know a lot, but that we do not practice the elementary things we do know. We should simplify the process and free disciple-making and multiplying for all Christians. Then we will be able to build on a solid foundation of spiritual growth.

What we need is a system that is practical and profound. It must be both simple and significant! A system that is significant enough to tap into the

Christian's internal motivation, yet simple enough that it can be easily passed on from disciple to disciple. Such a system will strengthen the church and produce growth that is qualitative and quantitative.

Paul could leave this planet victorious (2 Tim. 4:7-8) because he left behind someone who could carry the work to the next generation. We would all do well to ask ourselves, "If I were to die today, what of significance would I leave behind?" We should share Paul's concern for lasting influence and begin to invest in transformed disciples who can take the message of the gospel on to the next generation. Who is the Timothy in your life? Who will carry on after you've gone? Christianity's very survival depends on the lives that we leave behind, lives that have been changed and prepared to carry on beyond us.

Chapter 4:
Candidates for the Kingdom:
Where Do We Start?

Jesus told many parables of what the kingdom of God is like. One that stands out among the others is the parable of the sower. It is mentioned in three of the four gospels (Matt. 13:1-32; Luke 8:15; Mark 4:1-20). Jesus seems to indicate that our understanding of other parables hinges on us getting this one right (Mark 4:13). It is a foundational understanding of the kingdom of God.

In this parable Jesus describes how the kingdom of God spreads. He defines four kinds of soil, only one of which is good soil that brings forth fruit. The soils represent four kinds of souls. He defines the seed of the kingdom as the word of God (Luke 8:11).

What releases the life force that produces spontaneous growth and multiplication? Jesus taught that what is needed is the good seed in good soil. When this connection is made the life force is released and growth results naturally and spontaneously. The natural result of this growth is reproduction. In later chapters we will examine the role of God's word—the seed of His kingdom—in transforming a life. In this chapter we are asking the question—how do I determine what is good soil?

Jesus used the parable of the sower to teach us that good soil makes all the difference (Mark 4:1-8). Finding the right soul in which to plant the seed of the kingdom is of utmost importance to see life, growth and reproduction.

There are two criteria that aid in the discovery of good soil. They are what I use to test the soil before I invest time and energy into the disciple. While you may be able to start sooner with lesser criteria, you will not be able to see the long-lasting fruitfulness that Jesus speaks of with lesser criteria. It is well worth the wait in order to find someone who meets this simple yet significant standard.

1. People who desperately need Jesus (Luke 5:30-32).

Most discipleship programs today begin with saved people who either are already committed or want to be more committed. We often think that we should begin with the most committed people when we approach the disciple-making process. We believe that beginning with a better quality of people will assure us of greater success in the end. But in this sense, the kingdom of God is actually reversed. Jesus begins with those who most desperately need salvation. In Jesus' kingdom the losers become winners and those who appear to be winners end up last (Matt. 19:30; Mark 10:31; Luke 13:30).

Often we will avoid needy people for pragmatic reasons—they can be very demanding. Christian leaders even have terms for these people which we tend to keep secret by referring to them in acronyms Very Draining People are called VDP's, Extra Grace Required People are called EGR's. Have we actually developed a code for such people so that we can refer to them without exposing our true intent of avoiding them? Are we embarrassed by our lack of grace and compassion?

Most recommend that leaders not invest their time in these people because they are a losing proposition. And it is true that needy people can drain you if (a) they are not progressing and (b) the ministry is not equipped to provide adequate help. But if we don't help the needy, and we only focus on "healthy" people, we have missed the point of the church. The discipleship process must begin with people who have a real need for Christ.

There is a temptation to think that good people make good soil. In our church, however, we have a saying: Bad people make good soil! Fruitful plants tend to grow best where the fertilizer is abundant. Some people are drowning in fertilizer from poor decisions and acts of unrighteousness. We need to look for these people and begin to plant the seed of the kingdom there.

Regarding this Jesus said, "It is not those who are well who need a physician, but those who are sick. I have not come to call the righteous but sinners to repentance (Mark 2:17)."

It is quite refreshing to be able to offer immediate assistance to any who want help. In fact, needy people can actually be very refreshing to a busy Christian. When they see a life begin to change in radical ways they are reminded again of what Christianity is all about.

There are seven very important reasons that we must start the disciple-making process with people who desperately need Christ.

   a. Desperate sinners will hold onto Christ because their lives depend on it.

   b. Desperate sinners will see their lives change more readily than those who are already doing "well."

   c. Desperate sinners are more likely to confess their sin because it is more obvious.

   d. Desperate sinners will become walking and talking billboards to the power of the gospel to other desperate sinners.

   e. Desperate sinners usually have more contact with other desperate sinners who need Jesus.

   f. Desperate sinners are the very reason Jesus came and died. He delights to save them. Bring pleasure to your Master—give the gospel to a desperate sinner!

   g. Desperate sinners who are transformed by the gospel bring greater glory to God because it makes the miraculous that much more manifest. Only God could do such a miracle!

2. People who stay faithful to the process (2 Tim. 2:2).

This second point, while not obvious until the group begins, becomes the criterion for continuing the process.

Paul wrote to Timothy about passing on the baton, "these entrust to *faithful* men who will be able to teach others also (emphasis mine)." If the man or woman who has entered the group is not faithful to the disciple-making process, he or she will usually drop out. The group should not continue if the members are unwilling to continue with the process. This second criterion establishes the balance for the busy person who is concerned about being drained by a needy individual who doesn't really want to progress.

God Recycles for His Disciples

While these criteria may sound unorthodox they are really very Biblical. This has been the way of God from the beginning. God loves to recycle. He transforms garbage into glory. He turns trash into a triumph.

God chooses whom He uses, and most often the choice comes from those the world discounts. He loves to turn tax collectors into truth-givers and downcasts into disciples. He receives more glory when He uses weak things that amount to nothing, adds His presence and power and turns them into men or women of substance and even legend. Every one of His children should have the words stamped somewhere on their soul: "Made from 100% recycled material."

Here are just a few of the many examples one can find in the Scriptures.

First, let us consider David who, at a low point in his life, found himself alone in exile and seemingly out of place. He was a shepherd without a flock and king without a kingdom. Taking refuge in a cave, his family came to him. Then others followed. They were the outcasts, those who didn't fit in. 1 Samuel 22:2 describes them as,

> ... everyone who was in distress, and everyone who was in debt, and every one who was discontented, gathered to him; and he became captain over them. Now there were about four hundred men with him.

He was supposed to be a king. He became marshal of the misfits—regal of the rejects—emperor of the exiled. The people who nobody wanted to have around became the people David befriended. They lived together and fought together. They became a family, a tribe and eventually an army.

After that they were referred to as David and his men (1 Samuel 27:3-4, 8). Just by being with him, they were nobler; more wanted, more valuable. They also became fearless warriors.

As David rose in stature and fame, they also rose to high esteem and became legends who are still spoken of today. They became "the mighty men." They went from hopeless to heroes. Their acts of bravery would be known and read forever by all that would read the holy writ (2 Samuel 23:8-39).

Jesus also used the same criteria for choosing His men.

After a night of prayer, reflection and great consideration, Jesus chose twelve men to be His special disciples. He would leave His kingdom in the hands of these specially-chosen envoys. The only casting agency He looked to was the kind that had a worm on the end of the hook. The men He selected were not the most talented, good looking, wealthy, or educated. In fact, He was known for turning those away (Luke 18:18-27). He went for tax collectors, fishermen and zealots with an edge. They were outcasts and men of questionable reputation.

Jesus selected them and then spent time with them, trained them, mentored them and appointed them to lead (Mark 3:13-19).

These became the men who turned the Roman Empire on its head! These are the ones whose names will adorn the foundation stones of the new temple of God in New Jerusalem.

Finally, we need to look at Paul who also followed these same criteria in choosing those whom he would invest himself in. When he was in Cornith, the sin capitol of the Empire, Jesus told him, "I have many people in this city (Acts 18:10)." Paul made many disciples out of the sinners in that corrupt and immoral place. Eventually a church was born out of the darkness. Later, in a letter to them he would say,

> For consider your calling, brethren, that there were not many wise according to the flesh, not many mighty, not many noble; but God has chosen the foolish things of the world to shame the wise, and God has chosen the weak things of the world to shame the things which are strong, and the base things of the world and the despised, God has chosen, the things that are not, that He might nullify the things that are, that no man should boast before God (1 Cor. 1:26-29).

He would remind them of their humble beginnings by telling them,

> Or do you not know that the unrighteous shall not inherit the kingdom of God? Do not be deceived; neither fornicators, nor idolaters, nor adulterers, nor effeminate, nor homosexuals, nor thieves, nor the covetous, nor drunkards, nor revilers, nor swindlers, shall inherit the kingdom of God. And such were some of you; but you were washed, but you were sanctified, but you were justified in the name of the Lord Jesus Christ, and in the Spirit of our God (1 Cor. 6:9-11).

God delights in turning misfits into mighty men and zeroes into heroes. He is able to demonstrate so much more of His glorious attributes by doing such. His miraculous power is made obvious. His compassion is also shown when He takes a fisherman and makes him a foundation stone for a glorious kingdom. This is what the kingdom of God is all about and we need to get back to it.

44

If we get to thinking that it is our best assets that make us most valued to the Lord then we are close to being useless. We must become acquainted with our weaknesses if we are to see Him use us for great purposes. To those same Corinthian believers Paul later remarked,

> And He (Jesus) has said to me, 'My grace is sufficient for you, for my power is perfected in weakness.' Most gladly, therefore, I will rather boast about my weaknesses, that the power of Christ may dwell in me. Therefore I am well content with weaknesses, with insults, with distresses, with persecutions, with difficulties, for Christ's sake; for when I am weak, then I become strong (2 Cor. 12:9-10).

Chapter 5:
Breathing Life into New Disciples: Essential Ingredients to Transform Lives

In the same letter we looked at in the last chapter, which challenges Timothy to pass on the torch of faith to the succeeding generations, Paul tells Timothy and us that there are two essential disciplines necessary to make disciples who can be used by God. These are the disciplines needed to prepare ordinary people to do extraordinary work for the Lord. Both elements are necessary for effective disciple making. They go together and are as essential to the process as exhaling and inhaling are to breathing. In fact, they are much like breathing. They are the Cardio Pulmonary Resuscitation of people who need life. It is what gets their heart started for Jesus. It's as simple as "out with the bad air and in with the good."

1. Exhaling: the confession of sin (2 Tim. 2:19-22).

Paul wrote to Timothy:

> "Let everyone who names the name of the Lord abstain from wickedness." Now in a large house there are not only gold and silver vessels, but also vessels of wood and of earthenware, and some to honor and some to dishonor. Therefore if a man cleanses himself from these things, he will be a vessel of honor, sanctified, useful to the master, prepared for every good work.

The first discipline necessary for a disciple to grow into usefulness is the confession of sin. Unless we are cleansed from sin we will not be useful or honoring to the Lord. Christians are people of confession. John wrote, "If we confess our sins He is faithful and righteous to forgive us our sins and to cleanse us from all unrighteousness (1 John 1:9)." Without confession there is no cleansing. When we do confess our sins, we become cleansed and honorable, and our message becomes acceptable.

Paul likens us to vessels. By vessels, Paul means containers. Some are vessels of honor and some of dishonor. We all have daily contact with both kinds of vessels. A friend of mine is a plumber. He works with vessels of dishonor— the toilet. My dog may want to drink water from a toilet but I would never do so, it is a vessel of dishonor. My wife, Dana, and I have a weekly ritual every Thursday evening, which involves vessels of dishonor. After I settle down in bed and almost fall asleep she graciously reminds me that I need to take our two vessels of dishonor out to the curb so that the truck of dishonor can take the contents to the dump of dishonor.

To picture the difference between a vessel of honor and one of dishonor for my congregation, I once asked them to visualize two different vessels in my hands, both guaranteed to be sanitized and full of clean and cool water. One was a crystal goblet. The other a bed pan. No matter how clean it is, none of us would want to drink from a bedpan; it is a vessel of dishonor. But if you came to my home and I served you dinner with our fine china and crystal you would gladly receive it because it would be an honor. In fact, Dana and I have only used our china a few times since we were married which shows you how honored you would be. Paul is showing us, by this example, that when we are cleansed by confessing our sins we become vessels of honor and, as such, our message is more readily received.

King David, a man after God's heart, was not a perfect man. He sinned in some of the most notorious ways imaginable—adultery, murder, lies and cover-up. But he turned back to God. In his confession to God for his scandal in the Bathsheba fiasco, he said: "Create in me a clean heart O God, and renew a right spirit within me ... then I will teach transgressors Thy ways, and sinners will be converted to Thee (Psalm 51:10,13 NAS)." The way to have our message received by lost souls is to have our souls cleansed by confessing our sin.

Confession is verbal agreement. When the cops want a confession they are looking for the perpetrator to agree with the charges. When we confess our sins to God we are saying that we agree with Him that our sinful behavior is wrong and unholy.

There is also a place in the Christian life for confessing our sins with others of a common belief and purpose. James says that healing may come for us when we do so in a supportive environment of prayer (James 5:16).

Confessing sin regularly will make others more receptive to the message we bring! We often think that if we confess our inner secrets to others we will lose credibility in their eyes. Many have found, however, that the opposite is true. When we have the courage to confess our inadequacies we often gain credibility in the eyes of others because we demonstrate humility, honesty, and courage. We are seen as authentic, brave, and most of all, human. This will tend to raise us in stature not tear us down. It is important to do so in a safe place where confidentiality is a value, but often our fears of exposure are unwarranted. When there is no confession, there is suspicion and hypocrisy. People know that humans are fallible. When they pretend to not have faults, it raises suspicion, not credibility.

Do we really think that others believe that we don't sin? Do we really think that we can keep our masks on and fool people into thinking that we don't have temptations and flaws? Of course not. So when we do confess our sins it substantiates our authenticity rather than chipping away at our credibility. This is true especially when it comes to God. We can never fool Him with our masks. He knows how many hairs we have on our heads and He also knows what thoughts we have in them. We can hide nothing from almighty God. So when we confess our sins He isn't shocked.

There are no hidden scandals in heaven. When we confess our sins we don't embarrass God; in fact, we please Him. In the Psalm mentioned above, David writes, "Thou dost not delight in sacrifice, otherwise I would give it; Thou art not pleased with burnt offering. The sacrifices of God are a broken spirit; A broken and contrite heart O God, Thou wilt not despise."

When we confess our sins and are cleansed we become "useful to the Master, prepared for every good work."

2. Inhaling: receiving and obeying God's word (2 Tim. 3:16-17).

The second discipline needed to be useful to the Master is the regular intake of Scripture. Paul writes a little later in the passage:

All Scripture is inspired by God and profitable for teaching, for reproof, for correction, for training in righteousness that the man of God may be adequate, equipped for every good work.

The truth is clear, that it is the word of God that changes lives. It can keep us from sin (Psalm 119:9-11), it is what performs open-heart surgery on our souls so that we might be cured of our sin (Heb. 4:12), it provides us with direction (Ps. 119:105), and it is what sets us apart for God's purpose (John 17:17). We are foolish to think that we can equip people with less than the word of God. No amount of books, tools or sermons can replace a steady diet of God's word for equipping God's people.

When we confess our sins we exhale the bad air. When we read and meditate on the Scripture, we inhale the good air. Breathing requires both. Our cleansing from sin prepares us for every good work, while our reading of Scripture equips us for those works. One makes us ready to be used; the other gives us the equipment to do it. It is useless and even dangerous to have equipment that you are not prepared to use. But likewise, we cannot be effective by simply being prepared to do a job if we don't have the equipment to get it done.

Effective disciple making requires both of these disciplines working together to transform a life from the inside out.

Peter tells us,

> ... For you have been born again not of seed that is perishable but imperishable, that is, through the living and abiding word of God. ...Therefore, putting aside all malice and all guile and hypocrisy and envy and all slander, like newborn babes, long for the pure milk of the word, that by it you may grow in respect to salvation, if you have tasted the kindness of the Lord (1 Peter 1:23; 2:1-3).

Peter agrees with Paul on the two elements needed for growth in a disciple's life: continual cleansing from sin and a steady diet of God's word. There are, of course, several other spiritual disciplines that are needed for growth of the disciple such as prayer and worship. My purpose is not to exclude any others because they are obsolete or optional, but rather to present the two most essential elements needed to induce growth and multiplication. These two disciplines become the foundation for the others to be built upon.

Chapter 6:
The Best Context for Transforming Lives

Lives change in the context of community. There are no Lone Ranger Christians who are healthy believers. We need each other to stand against sin in our lives. In the passage we've been looking at in 2 Timothy, Paul says in verse 22, "Now flee from youthful lusts, and pursue righteousness, faith, love and peace, *with those who call on the Lord from a pure heart* (emphasis mine)." Note the use of the plural nouns in the verse we looked at earlier regarding multiplying disciples. Paul wrote, "And the things you have heard from me in the presence of many *witnesses*, these entrust to faithful *men*, who will be able to teach *others* also (emphasis mine)."

We need each other. Reproduction is always a cooperative effort—*it takes two to tango*! In almost all of nature two lives are needed to create another. When God created mankind, He created them male and female and He said, "Be fruitful and multiply and fill the earth." This is also His plan for His disciples, to be fruitful and multiply and fill the earth. Lives change when we are together in community.

I believe that the best context for life change is a community of two or three. Consistently throughout God's word there is reference to two or three. Here are five Biblical reasons why I think that a group of two or three is the best context for disciple making and multiplying:

1. Community

Ecclesiastes 4:9-12 says, "Two are better than one because they have a good return for their labor. For if either of them falls, the one will lift up his companion. But woe to the one who falls when there is not another to lift him up. Furthermore, if two lie down together they keep warm, but how can one be warm alone? And if one can overpower him who is alone, two can resist him. A cord of three strands is not quickly torn apart."

Life change does not occur in a vacuum; it happens in relationship with others. From the beginning, God has said, "It is not good for man to be alone." God designed us with a need for community.

While a community can be a larger group than three, a group of three can be the strongest form of community. For most, it is difficult to have the kind of close-knit relational bond that can change our life with more than three people at any one time. The best context for a life-changing community is in a group of two or three.

Three, in fact, is the ideal number for a group to experience real growth through community. With a group of three it is harder for one person to dominate the discussion (though not impossible). It is also harder for someone to hide in a group of three. It is easier to have full participation from all in a group of only three, but as the size of the group increases, some become more outspoken and others fade into the background.

2. Accountability

1 Timothy 5:19 says, "Do not receive an accusation against an elder except on the basis of two or three witnesses."

Few things would ever get done in life without some degree of accountability. In the pursuit of godliness we need accountability to one another. There are at least 28 "one another" admonitions in the New Testament. Many more if you count those which are repeated. We need each other.

It is difficult to be held accountable to a multitude of people who do not know you well. A group of two or three has a greater degree of strength in accountability. One can find support with a group of two or three who know and understand his or her life.

3. Confidentiality

Matthew 18:15-17 says, "And if your brother sins, go and reprove him in private; if he listens to you, you have won your brother. But if he does not listen to you, take one or two more with you, so that by the mouth of two or three witnesses every fact may be confirmed. And if he refuses to listen to them, tell it to the church."

Since confession of sin is needed for cleansing and preparing one for a life of service, then a safe place is essential. Rarely do people feel comfortable confessing their sins to a large group filled with people they don't know. A small/cell group, which is coed, is also not a safe enough place to share your darkest secrets. A group of two or three others of your same gender, who know and care about you and who also are sharing their own struggles is as safe a place as one can find.

Confidentiality is much easier to control in a context of two or three. This is especially true when each participant is vulnerable and equally at risk of exposure. If confidentiality is indeed broken there is a short list of suspects to consider.

The Lord specifically indicated that it is best to have a group of two or three when confronting sin in order to maintain confidentiality (Matt. 18:15-17).

4. Flexibility

Matthew 18:20 says, "For where two or three have gathered together in My name, there I am in their midst."

Certainly there is more behind the words Jesus spoke in the above verse, but flexibility is one advantage of a group this size.

Most of us have had the experience of trying to coordinate the calendars of a handful of busy people. An advantage to a group of two or three is that there is a better opportunity to coordinate schedules for a meeting time for all.

A second logistical advantage to a group of two or three is that they can meet almost anywhere. We have had some groups meet in a restaurant for coffee, some meet in a gym while working out, others have met at the park where their children can play and they can walk together. There is no need for a host/hostess with this size of group.

5. Reproducibility

As we have already mentioned, simple things multiply easier than complex things. A group of two or three can multiply much easier than a small/cell group of ten to fifteen. All that is needed to multiply such a group is to find one more person and multiply into two groups of two. If we cannot see multiplication at this level, we will not see it at higher, more complex levels of church life. If we can't multiply groups of two or three we will not multiply a cell group, or a worship service or a congregation.

This is the most basic unit of the church—two or three believers held together by the presence of Jesus Christ and the truth of His word. By initiating multiplication here, at the base unit, we can infuse the very genetic code of the church with the value of reproduction. If we truly wish to see the power of multiplication released in our church it is best to initiate the momentum here at the grassroots level.

Church planting is my calling and passion. It dawned on me one day, however, that I could not find a single verse in all the Bible which commands us to plant or multiply churches. It's just not there! The command that God gave us was to make and multiply disciples, not cell groups or churches. Jesus does want to build His kingdom through church planting and multiplication, but His plan is to do so by multiplying disciples. It begins here—with the basic unit of the church then it spreads through every pore in the body of Christ. But, if we do not start here, if we skip this God-ordained step, we can work and work and work until we turn blue and drop dead and we will not see multiplication happen.

The diagram on page 53 gives you a visual example of how multiplication can emerge in a church from the grassroots disciple-making level.

If none of the evidence listed above is enough to convince you of the Biblical precedent for groups of two or three then this last reason is sure to clench the debate. Even the Godhead exists in a community of three! I only half joke about this. Jesus used the community of the Godhead to teach us how we are to function together (John 17:11, 21). Perhaps there really is something special, even spiritual, about a group of two or three.

ORGANIC CHURCH REPRODUCTION WITH LIFE TRANSFORMATION GROUPS

LIFE TRANSFORMATION GROUPS

SEED IN SOIL:
Making and Multiplying Disciples

CELL GROUPS

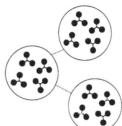

DEVELOPMENT OF A BODY:
Multiplying Groups

CONGREGATIONS OF GROUPS

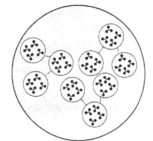

A FULLY FUNCTIONING BUT IMMATURE BODY:
Multiplying Ministries

NEW CHURCH PLANTING CHURCHES

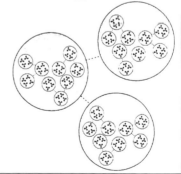

REPRODUCING OF THE BODY:
Multiplying Churches

Chapter 7:
Living Examples—
Our Story

Designing a disciple-making system with all the above principles in mind would be an ambitious project. Only by God's grace did we stumble upon a method that encompassed all of these principles. I feel there is a sense in which God is the designer of the system and we merely discovered it. That is not to say that this is the only system that works but merely to emphasize that God was gracious in leading us to discover a simple way to multiply growing disciples. I will share with you how we came upon the system and how lives have been touched as a result. I have changed the names of the people I am writing about but the stories themselves are all true.

I have always had a drive to make disciples and have always had multiplication as a value in disciple-making. I have used many of the materials and curriculum available, some with more success than others. Every system that I used failed in one way or another. They would often get boring to me after one or two times through the material. Once the leader was bored the group was doomed. I also found that none of the materials would reproduce well. Rarely did I see multiple generations of reproduction.

One common problem of discipleship systems available today is that the leader often feels that he/she is not being adequately nourished and resourced. Meeting is piled upon meeting to make sure that every level of the system is being helped, and soon leadership becomes too time costly. The alternative is for the leaders not to be fed themselves, which is not an adequate solution either. A leader is one who influences a group. A leader by very definition leads. Once the leader stops growing he or she will lead the group toward stagnation and mediocrity.

I eventually resorted to reading the newest and best books with my groups and then discussing the reading together once a week. I was in the midst of a very good book by Chuck Swindoll when I started to get bored again. I wasn't bored with the book, I just didn't see the lives of my disciples changing as a result. One of the guys in the group had an obvious problem with anger and the book was just not getting through. Finally, I decided that we would try the Bible and I told the group, "Put away the book we've been reading, or read it on your own. This week I want you to read Proverbs." They thought they were getting off the hook, so they were excited. Then they asked which Proverbs I wanted them to read. Their countenance changed quickly when I said, "All of them." "In a week?" one asked. "Yes, 31 chapters in a week." I figured that if Solomon and the Holy Spirit couldn't teach this young man how to deal with his anger, then nothing that I or even Chuck Swindoll could say would help.

When we got together the next week, I discovered that the guys were not taking me too seriously and were testing my resolve. While I had finished the reading, the next closest to completing the reading was at about chapter 12. Because I didn't think that they gave the Scripture a chance, and partly because they didn't take me seriously, I told them, "OK, we're going to read Proverbs again. And if any one of you doesn't finish the reading, we will read it again, and again until we all show up at the same time with the reading done."

Four weeks later we had all finished reading Proverbs. One of us had read the book four times in four weeks. It felt like a breath of fresh air had come across my face. This was exciting and powerful. This was a means of feeding myself as much as my disciples.

Unfortunately, my friend still had an anger problem so I thought I would continue to turn up the heat with more Scripture. They all seemed excited when they had finished reading Proverbs, so I said, "Let's not stop, lets read James seven times this week. Again, we won't move on until all of us finish the reading together." At this point things in the group began to change. One man began to take a turn toward other things. He didn't want to admit to himself that this was the case so he refused to stop being a part of our group, but he would never finish the reading. As a result of his flakiness, we read James 49 times before we were finally able to move on. After we finally finished reading James, the man who was holding us back decided that this group was not for him.

At the same time, the man who had an anger problem decided that he didn't want to continue with the reading, the group, or our church, so he stopped coming. His girlfriend also stopped coming. Just when I felt an excitement for disciple-making again, the group died. But at the same time, God brought a new man into the kingdom and into my group. His name was Marty.

Marty had been living a self-destructive life as an alcoholic and was experimenting with drugs. When I first met Marty, his parents were in our church but he was caught in the world. He'd already been in jail, had a couple D.U.I.'s, had his driver's license suspended and an accident. He came to church one morning when I was preaching a message on the consequences of sin, and I could tell that the Spirit was convicting him. After the message, I immediately walked up to him and asked if he wanted to join our discipleship group. I was determined not to accept any answer but yes, because I could sense that God was working in his heart. He told me that he couldn't join us because he couldn't drive due to a suspended license. I told him I would pick him up at 5:45 a.m. Wednesday morning. He agreed. I arrived at 5:45 and honked my horn. After getting dressed he joined me and we went to the group together. After a few weeks of reading the Bible, Marty began to have a change of heart. He became a new creation, old things began to pass away as new things began to emerge. He asked if he could be baptized again (he was baptized in junior high). He felt that he was experiencing such a change of life that a baptism was in order and I obliged gladly.

Four other young people, Henry, Randy, Heather and Veronica began meeting with us and we soon outgrew the booth we were sitting at in the restaurant and needed to move to a larger booth. The entire group was changed and was now made up of motivated people.

The Bible reading was beginning to have an effect on our lives. We settled into a pattern of reading about thirty chapters of the Bible each week. We continued the accountability to finish together in order to move on to another book.

Until that time, I usually would read the passage that I was to preach that week for my devotional times. Or, another way to put it, I would study for my sermons instead of having a devotional. Don't get me wrong, the Scriptures would impact my life and in so doing bring a freshness to my sermons and make them very personal. But when we began reading so much Scripture, I knew that I would have to read a designated portion of Scripture each day apart from the text that I was preaching from if I had any hope at all of keeping up with the group.

I began to hear from God in my Bible reading and developed a great appetite for Scripture. Marty and the others did as well. After a couple of months this way, someone approached me after church on Sunday and asked me a question that sent me into a discovery process. He said, "Hey Neil, what are you doing differently? Whatever it is, it's working. Keep doing it. Your preaching is so much more powerful."

This intrigued me and I began to ask myself why. The answer was that I was infused so much more with Scripture that my preaching was bound to be affected. I began to wonder what other ways these groups would affect our church. From that point on, I began to look at the group with the eye of an explorer. I was in a discovery process so I began journaling and taking down observations. I was on a quest. The book you now hold in your hands is the discovery of my quest.

One of the first things I noticed was that the group would start to grow and just when I expected us to break loose and need to rent a meeting room, it would dwindle back down to three. A short time later, it would begin to grow and again it would come back down to three. It would never die—it just wouldn't grow beyond three. The enthusiasm would never diminish, lives didn't stop changing, but the numbers would not grow as I had expected.

Finally, I listened to the Lord and figured out what He was trying to tell me. The group had a natural size that worked best. Rather than force the group to be something unnatural, I decided to keep the group limited to three, and then multiply. The results made an immediate impact on the groups. Within one year that one group became approximately ten groups! It is possible that there were as many as twenty groups in our church the following year.

Marty's growth continued as he was reading the Bible and making applications to his life. He developed relationships at church. He went back to school. I began encouraging Marty to share his newfound faith with those he used to party with. Though he never would say so, he was less than enthusiastic about bringing up Christ with his old drinking buddies. I wanted him to do so before the relational ties became cold and the opportunity was lost.

Marty's best friend was not a Christian. They continued to have fun together as buddies. One day they decided to go into business together. To celebrate, they went out to dinner. Marty's friend ordered two margaritas and had them set down before them. Marty resisted at first, reminding his friend that he doesn't drink anymore. But his friend persisted, insisting that they celebrate together like the good old days. Marty gave in and had one drink. Then another, and another and sure enough, they were back to the "good" old days. Late that night they were driving home in Marty's truck. Marty was not driving because his license was still suspended.

They were driving up a hill and approaching an intersection when the light turned red. Marty said to his friend, "Go for it, you'll make it." They didn't. Their truck was hit directly on the driver's side by a car heading east. When Marty awoke the truck was on his arm, glass was all over the place and the paramedics were preparing to fly him via helicopter to an emergency trauma center. He later found out that his friend was killed instantly.

I received the call that Marty was hurt early that morning. I immediately drove out to see him. He still had glass and dried blood in his hair, but he was going to fully recover. He lost some feeling in his arm, but the doctors suspected that he would regain full use of it, and he did.

We talked a little. He was still shaken. I knew that this was a significant moment in Marty's life so I chose my words carefully. I looked him in the eye and asked him, "Marty, what do you think God is trying to tell you?" With his lip quivering and his eyes full of tears, He looked up at me and said, "I just can't believe that my best friend is in hell right now and there is nothing that I can do about it."

Marty would never be the same again. From that day on he has been sober and has had a heart to share the gospel with those around him. One day, while skiing with friends from college, he met a pretty girl who wasn't a Christian. He thought she was cute, but he knew he couldn't date a non-Christian, so he led her to Christ and then they began dating. After Kathy received the Lord she quickly began to grow in her new faith. Eventually they were married and together they make a dynamic team. Kathy began meeting with another growing believer in our church—Heather. Another young woman accepted Christ, was baptized, and joined their group. Soon after the group multiplied.

Both Marty and Kathy have a heart for sharing the gospel with the lost that flows from their own salvation experience. Marty has become the youth pastor at church. He has a passion for reaching young troubled teens that are in the same bondage he was released from.

I learned many valuable things from Marty. I saw a need to introduce an element of accountability to our meetings. I began to ask him each week, "So how many days of sobriety has it been so far?" This was my way of (not so) subtly holding him accountable. Eventually I started asking, "Have you given in to a personal addiction this week? Explain." I did this because I have found that people with addictive behaviors can often find other means of falling into bondage. To God's glory Marty did not.

I also found the need to integrate accountability for evangelism into our meetings.

I had been studying John Wesley and the beginning of the Methodist movement. They used to ask one another accountability questions in small groups to keep in touch with each other and to keep one another accountable for their spiritual growth. At that same time I was reading *The Body*, by Charles Colson. In it he gives an example of some questions that Chuck Swindoll used to keep himself accountable with other pastors.

I took those questions, adapted them, added a few more and came up with a list of accountability questions. The questions have been adapted and altered several times since, but they have always been a simple way to hold one another accountable. They allow us to confess our sins to one another without feeling like we are intruding into personal areas that are none of our business. With the introduction of these questions I knew it would be necessary to keep the groups of a single gender rather than coed. I encouraged the women to begin groups of their own. I also challenged them to come up with questions that relate best with their own needs, which they did. Eventually, the questions settled down to a list that can be appropriate for both sexes. Once I started using the Accountability Questions, I saw the multiplication begin.

At first I wasn't even expecting the groups to multiply. I was having a nice time alone at the restaurant where my group met. Our usual waitress came up to me and said, "You'd be really proud of Marty." I said, "I am, but why do you think that I should?" She said, "His group is doing real well." I was puzzled and asked, "Marty has a group?" She said, "Yeah, every Monday morning they have more and more young people who are excited about learning the Bible." This is how I found out that my group had multiplied.

Soon after, Marty left that group and began another. The first group he had started went on without him to give birth to three or four others and eventually became the foundation of a new ministry to young singles.

A short time later another man, Bob, came to me with marital problems and asked if I could help. I suggested that we start a meeting together for this kind of accountability, saying, "If confessing our sins together, and reading the Bible doesn't help, there's nothing my counsel will be able to do."

This man took instantly to the system. His marriage began to improve as his own heart and mind were being cleansed and renewed. His wife also began an accountability group. This couple had been attending our church for a while, but they never got involved much. Suddenly they were volunteering for ministry and developing a compassion for the lost. They brought several couples into the church. He led a man and his wife to the Lord, who in turn brought another couple to church who accepted Christ. We had a grand baptism made up of three generations of conversion growth. He began meeting with these men and our group multiplied. I in turn began meeting with another man, Frank, who likewise was having marital problems. This multiplication took place only four months after my initial meeting with Bob.

Frank came to my office in desperate need. After only a year of marriage he suspected his wife was cheating on him. He was a broken man who would do anything to get his life and marriage back on track. I asked him if he would begin meeting with me on Saturday mornings and he eagerly accepted. So we began the same weekly accountability mentioned above. Because of his desperation, Frank was faithful and eager in the process and the fruit of that faithfulness bore immediate results. His own life began to transform. As God's word became real to him for the first time, he learned the value of confessing his own sin and taking responsibility for his own life choices.

I wasn't the only one who was noticing the growth in his character. Frank's wife also noticed. At first this was difficult. They ended up separating for a time without any promise of reconciliation, yet he continued in his newfound spiritual discovery regardless of the way his marriage would turn out. He may have begun the accountability for the sake of his wife, but in the process he fell in love with Jesus and he would continue with or without her.

A short time into these Saturday morning meetings Jim came to me tired of living a life in spiritual complacency and carnality. He was ready to grow, so I asked him to join Frank and I. He took readily to the process and immediately began to grow.

Within a year this group multiplied into three groups, mostly through real conversion growth. Frank ended up leading his father and brother to Christ and baptized them on a very special Sunday. The three of them became a group of their own. Frank's wife came back to Christ and to her husband. I heard that even her lover accepted Jesus and began attending another church! Frank went on to start a business of his own which had as a goal to employ church planters and pastors in such a way that they could stay home, work a few hours and make enough income to invest the time needed to begin a new church. The business is only in the embryonic stage at the time of this writing, but the idea is certainly viable and demonstrates the kind of passion for the kingdom birthed in his heart.

Jim also began a group when another man accepted Christ, was baptized and immediately plugged into this revolutionary discipleship process.

With Frank and Jim both starting groups of their own it was time for me to also birth a new group. My next group is the only one of our three that wasn't the result of conversion growth, but it was amazingly powerful nonetheless.

After seeing the dramatic changes in people's lives through this disciple-making process, a couple of the key leaders in my church asked me if I could do the same with them. Apparently the Lord had stirred up a godly jealousy in some of the elders in our church and who was I to deny these good men the blessings others had enjoyed. I began meeting with these two men on Saturday mornings. Within a year, one had given over his own business to the Lord, devoting it to employing bivocational church planters and accepting a call himself to become a worship leader in our church. At the time of this writing he has employed several of our youth pastors and three tent-making church planters.

The other elder whom I began meeting with also felt a new call of God upon his life. He had a dramatic sense of calling to ministry which eventually led to his becoming the pastor to take over the leadership of the church after my own departure to begin a new church planting work. This call is explained further in a later chapter of this book.

This one Saturday morning meeting, which began with a man in desperate need of help, grew and multiplied leading six people to the Lord, two men to devote their businesses to further the kingdom, at least one man into the pastorate and another to church planting. All this took place in less than two years time.

Chapter 8:
The Life Transformation Groups System

In this section I will explain how the system works and then examine the advantages and most common objections to it.

The Life Transformation Group (LTG) system is a grass-roots tool for growth. Through this simple system the most essential elements of vital spiritual ministry are released to common Christians without the need for specialized training. It taps the disciple's internal motivation and provides the support needed to grow in the essentials of a spiritual life. The LTG empowers the common Christian to do the uncommon work of reproductive discipling.

An LTG is made up of two to three people, all of the same gender, who meet weekly for personal accountability in the areas of their spiritual growth and development. A group should not grow beyond three but multiply into two groups of two rather than a single group of four. If a fourth person is added to the group it is recommended that the group consider itself pregnant and ready to give birth to a second group. Once the fourth person has demonstrated sufficient faithfulness (2-3 weeks) then the group should multiply into two groups of two.

There is no curriculum or training needed for the LTG. A simple bookmark which stays in the participant's Bible is all that is needed.

The LTG accountability consists of three essential disciplines for personal spiritual growth—a steady diet of Scripture, confession of sin and prayer for others who need Christ.

1. Sin is Confessed

The first thing the LTG does together at a meeting is ask one another the accountability questions found on one side of the LTG Bible bookmark. The meetings should always begin with this because it is easy to get lost in conversation and run out of time for the questions. Beginning each meeting with the confession of sin tends to sanctify the rest of the time together. The questions are straightforward. Each person in the group takes a turn answering each question honestly. The group must be a safe place where the participants feel they can be honest and vulnerable. This is the reason why coed groups do not work well. The questions are as follows:

1. Have you been a testimony this week to the greatness of Jesus Christ with both your words and actions?

2. Have you been exposed to sexually alluring material or allowed your mind to entertain inappropriate thoughts about someone who is not your spouse this week?

3. Have you lacked any integrity in your financial dealings this week, or coveted something that does not belong to you?

4. Have you been honoring, understanding and generous in your important relationships this past week?

5. Have you damaged another person by your words, either behind their back or face-to-face?

6. Have you given in to an addictive behavior this week? Explain.

7. Have you continued to remain angry toward another?

8. Have you secretly wished for another's misfortune so that you might excel?

9. Your personal accountability question _____

10. Did you finish your reading this week and hear from the Lord? What are you going to do about it?

11. Have you been completely honest with me?

The accountability questions are designed in such a way as to bring to remembrance any sin that may need to be confessed. The system is meant to bc simple and transferable so that anyone can apply it. We have worked through many drafts of questions to find a simple list that can cover a broad scope of behavior that needs regular confession.

There is, however, a potential danger inherent with the questions that I want to make clear. It is important for those who are involved with an LTG to submit to the spirit of the system more than the letter of the law. These questions are meant to stimulate discussion and open sharing but they are not in themselves an exhaustive list of all that sin is, nor do they define what true righteousness is. Simply adhering to the behavior promoted in these questions does not necessarily solidify one's righteousness. Certainly obedience and the confession of sin can lead to righteousness, but we dare not believe that this list of questions is the standard of all that is righteousness. Jesus Himself is the standard of righteousness (Matt. 5:17-20; John 5:39-47). We must follow Jesus, not a list of questions if we want to pursue righteousness. The questions we have given as samples are only tools to help you in your pursuit of Jesus—the *only* Savior of our sins.

Another reason why these questions alone are insufficient to establish righteousness in our lives is that most of us have enough creativity in our flesh to find ways to sin which are not covered by these questions.

These questions have proven very helpful in uncovering sinful patterns that need to be openly confessed in a safe and healing community. The LTG provides a wonderful place to be accountable to overcome patterns of sinful behavior.

There are, however, other alternatives to do the same thing. I have always said that people should feel free to adjust the questions to be of the most personal benefit. Some use questions that are more open-ended and less specific. For example, one pastor I know uses questions similar to the following in his LTG's:

1. How has God made His presence known to you this week?

2. What is God teaching you?

3. How are you responding to His prompting?

4. Is there someone you need to share Christ with this next week?

5. Do you have a need to confess any sin?

These questions are simple and transferable, yet they allow for a much broader application and openness to the leading of the Spirit in a person's life. The advantage of the accountability questions previously listed above is that they bring to light more specific behaviors that may need to be confessed but which may have gone forgotten otherwise. They are a more thorough inventory to process one's life with. Both have advantages and disadvantages and either will accomplish the goal if applied in the proper spirit.

I have included an appendix that lists a variety of lists of questions used for accountability. Use whatever works best for you. I only have three suggestions in this regard. First, that you somehow include in your list of questions one that holds the group members accountable to openly sharing a testimony of Christ's goodness with others. It should be something that goes beyond living as an example but also includes a verbal witness. I would also suggest that you have at least one question that asks each person in the group if they are listening to the Lord and responding. Finally, I would also suggest that confessing of sin be a part of the accountability process.

The goal of having accountability is not just sin management but rather to foster an honest relationship that is transparent, caring and where healing can come through the confession of sin.

The confessing of sin cleanses and prepares the soul for every good work God has for him or her. While confession cleanses us from all unrighteousness (1 John 1:9) it alone does not produce righteousness in us. That is why the second discipline of the LTG is so important—the intake of God's word.

2. Scripture is Planted

The power of the LTG system lies in the unleashing of God's word into the lives of people. The Lord made it clear that the word of God is the seed of new life. He said, "Now the parable is this: the seed is the word of God. And the seed in the good soil, these are the ones who have heard the word in an honest and good heart, and hold it fast, and bear fruit with perseverance (Luke 8:11, 15)."

Each group agrees on a book of the Bible to be read. Sometimes an introductory reading schedule is used to help get things started. The goal is to have the people reading larger volumes of Scripture repetitively and in a whole context.

For a steady diet, I strongly recommend reading 25 to 30 chapters each week. If the book agreed upon is a shorter book, such as Ephesians or Jonah, it is read five to seven times in a week. If the book is a moderate size, such as 1 Corinthians or Romans, it is read twice in a week. If the book is longer than that, such as Proverbs, Revelation or Acts, the book is read once a week.

Books that are even longer, such as Genesis, Psalms or Isaiah can be broken up. Use natural breaks if possible. Each section can be read as you would the shorter books mentioned above. For example, Genesis can be broken into three sections: chapters 1-12; chapters 13-35; and chapters 36-50. Each section can be read twice in a week. Another example is to break Genesis down into two groups of 25 chapters and read each section once in a week. There is no set pattern, only a goal of reading twenty five to thirty chapters of Scripture per week. Some books have shorter chapters which can mean reading an increased number per week. Psalms, for example, can be read in two parts of 75 chapters in a week.

Sometimes, sections of books can be read repetitively. We have read Matt. 5-7 (the Sermon on the Mount) seven times in a week and found it to be very powerful. Psalm 119 can be approached that way as can Jesus' letters to the seven churches of Asia Minor in Revelation two and three. The key is to choose a section that forms a natural unit and read it enough that you are reading approximately thirty chapters in a week.

When the LTG meets the following week they ask one another if the entire reading was completed in time (number 9 of the accountability questions). If any one of the group was unable to complete the reading portion, then the same reading assignment is to be taken up again. The LTG will continue reading the same portion of Scripture repeatedly until the group finishes it together in the same week. Once all group members finish the reading in the same week, then a new book is agreed upon for the next week. Group members can rotate the privilege of choosing the next book to read if so desired.

It is important to note that it is not a failure for someone to be unable to complete the reading in a given week. In fact, it is advantageous if that happens. It is best if it takes a few weeks to get through a book because the repetition helps in the understanding and application of the truth. For this reason, we suggest that the amount of Scripture chosen to be read be a stretch for the group to finish. If a group finishes the designated amount each week then they are probably not reading enough and need to increase the volume. If the group is reading over thirty chapters every week, and they manage to finish the assigned reading every week, it is not enough and the group needs to increase the amount of reading. Ideally, it should average about three to four weeks for the group to complete the assignment.

In my own experience, on the weeks when any one of us fails to complete the reading, we feel that the Lord is not done teaching us something in that particular book. We then go into the next week with anticipation, believing that the Holy Spirit has a special lesson in store for us. We are never disappointed.

This form of accountability is a breath of fresh air in this highly segregated and individualistic society we live in. A major weakness of the Western church is the independent and individualistic approach to spiritual development. In the Eastern world, the ideas of family and community are stronger. It is interesting to note how cell-based ministry and multiplication is occurring more easily in cultures which naturally understand community as opposed to the Western world which prizes the individual over community. This affects all areas of the church. The LTG's, in Biblical fashion, operate naturally in community. We stay together. We learn together. We move forward together. Our spiritual growth is tied to others in a natural bond (Eph. 4:11-16). We care about one another's progress. In a sense, we learn to love one another as ourselves. My progress is tied to my brother's, and vice versa. This sanctified peer pressure works to stimulate growth in one another. Like a team, as each player improves, the ability of the entire team is raised to another level, far beyond any individual effort alone.

God has always intended for His people to work as a team. He wrote in Hebrews 10:24-25:

> And let us consider how to stimulate one another to love and
> good deeds, not forsaking our own assembling together, as is
> the habit of some, but encouraging one another; and all the more,
> as you see the day drawing near.

The LTG can be a first step for the Westerner to learn what community really is. Groups can then be built on transformed lives that have discovered the true value of community in an LTG.

3. Souls are Strategically Prayed For

The Accountability Questions are printed on a card to be used as a bookmark in the Bible (provided on the back cover of this book). On the reverse side of the card is the Strategic Prayer Focus. This is designed to be a reminder to pray strategically for lost people every time the Bible is opened (which is frequently in this system).

Each member of the LTG is to identify the two or three people who are the highest evangelistic priorities that God has laid on their hearts. They share the names of these people at a group meeting and each writes the names down on the card in the spaces provided. Each person should have listed all the names represented in the group, totaling six names. Each time one of us does our Bible reading we select one of the names and pray for that person using the suggested prayer guide. With this system, the person who is targeted for strategic prayer is prayed for two to three times by two or three different people every week. The prayers (listed below) that are offered are specific, progressive and extensive. They are also in accordance with Biblical principles of prayer and the salvation of lost souls.

1. I pray Lord, that You draw _____ to Yourself (John 6:44).

2. I pray that _____ seek to know You (Acts 17:27).

3. I pray that _____ hear and believe the Word of God (1 Thess. 2:13).

4. I ask You to prevent Satan from blinding _____ to the truth (2 Cor. 4:4; 2 Tim. 2:25-26).

5. Holy Spirit, I ask You to convict _____ of his/her sin and his/her need for Christ's redemption.

6. I ask You to send someone who will share the gospel with _____ (Matt. 9:37-38).

7. I also ask that You give me (and/or my fellow disciple) the opportunity, the courage and the right words to share the truth with _____ (Col. 4:3-6; Eph. 6:19-20).

8. Lord, I pray that _____ turn from his/her sin (Acts 17:30-31; 1 Thess. 1:9-10).

9. Lord, I pray that _____ would put all of his/her trust in Christ (John 1:12; 5:24).

10. Lord, I pray that _____ confess Christ as Lord of his/her life, take root and grow in his/her faith and bear much fruit for Your glory (Rom. 10:9-10; Col. 2:6-7; Luke 8:15).

It is a group effort in bringing these souls before the throne of grace. When we see a new soul born into the kingdom we all rejoice, having played a significant role in the process. Those who come to faith in Christ as a result of these prayers can form the next group, and multiplication can occur naturally, spontaneously and in a manner that the whole group rejoices in.

Summary of the System

The LTG system is simple, yet powerful. It incorporates the values of community, life transformation and reproduction of disciples. At our church there is a place for anyone who wants to grow in Christ. There is no need for a new Christian to wait for a class to open. There is no ceiling to the care we can offer because the groups can multiply quickly and easily to accommodate any number the Lord grants us. The usual barriers do not limit us. We truly have a sense that we can provide help to any that have a need, whenever they have a need. If the Lord chose to bless us with a large number of new conversions, we would be able to be responsible for their spiritual growth and development.

Let's summarize:

a. LTG's meet once a week for approximately an hour.

b. LTG's are groups of two or three (the 4th person is the beginning of the second group and multiplication is imminent).

c. The groups are not coed.

d. There is no curriculum, workbook or training involved.

e. There is no leader needed in the group.

f. Only three tasks are to be accomplished:

1) Sin is confessed to one another in mutual accountability.

2) Scripture is read repetitively, in entire context and in community.

3) Souls are prayed for strategically, specifically and continuously.

Chapter 9:
Advantages of the
LTG System

A Parable for the Church Today

There is a stranger-than-fiction phenomenon occurring in our world today and it provides a scary parable for the Western church. It is an unnatural mutation affecting a variety of species in the wild, and may ultimately be affecting humans. This mutation is not noticeable without careful observation, but affects the reproductive life of creatures and can potentially render some species extinct.

Sounding more like an episode for the Outer Limits than reality, the effects of this phenomenon can be horrifying. It is now a grave global concern for environmentalists and should be of concern to all of us. I do not raise this merely to alert us to an environmental crisis, but as a parable to help explain why the Western church today runs the risk of extinction and finds herself virtually infertile and incapable of reproducing.

The following story is taken directly from an article in the *Los Angeles Times* titled, "Hormone Disrupters Cause Sterility." The article was printed on Sunday, October 2, 1994 and carried the following sub-heading: "Sexual Confusion In The Wild: From gators to gulls, scientists say pollution may be playing havoc with animals hormones. Some males try to lay eggs; some females nest together. Certain species may risk extinction."

It reads,

> In the gender bending waters of Lake Apopka, alligators aren't quite male. They aren't quite female either. They may be both. Or neither. This sexual confusion in the wild, discovered in the steamy Florida swamp last year, is so disturbing to scientists

that they keep performing test after test on the scaly reptiles trying to prove themselves wrong. But the more they look, the more evidence they find. In fact, hardly any young alligators with normal sexuality can be found in this vast lake on the suburban outskirts of Orlando.

Elsewhere around the world, the same astonishing phenomenon is turning up in a menagerie of fish, birds and other wild animals. Testosterone levels have plummeted in some males, while females are supercharged with estrogen. Both sexes sometimes are born with a male and female reproductive organs, and some males wind up so gender warped that they try to produce eggs.

"Everything is really fouled up It is indeed real, and it is very scary," said Tim Gross, a University of Florida wildlife endocrinologist on the team that discovered the feminized alligators. "We didn't want to believe it, in all honesty."

Wildlife scientists have uncovered persuasive evidence that artificial pesticides and industrial chemicals are infiltrating wombs and eggs, where they send false signals imitating or blocking hormones, which control sexuality. Although the parents are unharmed, their embryo's sexual development is disrupted, and some male offspring are left chemically castrated and females sterile. The potential consequences, if unabated, are unthinkable. If males aren't male and females aren't female, they cannot reproduce and some outwardly healthy populations could be a generation away from extinction.

The ability of these chemicals, called endocrine disrupters, to leave the parents unharmed but afflict the unborn is alarming.

"Its the hand-me-down poison, from parents to offspring," said World Wildlife Fund senior scientist Teo Colborn.

The most insidious aspect is that the damage easily goes undetected; the animals look healthy, even to experts. Their bizarre sexuality is discovered only if their internal genitalia are examined or their hormones are tested."[21]

What would you think if 85-90 percent of the women in our country were infertile and incapable of giving birth? Would you be concerned for the health of these people? Would you be concerned for the future of our nation? Of course you would. So why are we not concerned when 85-90 percent of our churches are infertile and not giving birth to new churches?

The church today suffers a similar crisis to the alligators in Lake Apopka. Churches may appear healthy, but they are unable to reproduce, which threatens the viability of the church to carry on to the next generation. In this chapter we will discover that one reason that she is infertile is because she is being fed a seed substitute, which acts much like a hormone disrupter, and she has been rendered sterile.

The simple and yet significant ingredients found in the LTG system can bring health and fertility back to the bride. The LTG system itself is not a solution for all that ails a church, nor is it the agent of transformation of lives, ministries and churches. Lives are never really changed by any system or methodology. The Holy Spirit and the word of God working in a life that's cleansed and open to obey are what bring about transformation. The system itself is not what sanctifies and regenerates a soul.

A catalyst is not the ingredient that hardens the varnish or glue, but it accelerates the properties that are already inherent in the other ingredients. In a like manner, the LTG system is really just a catalyst that brings together the properties that cause change, into a relational context that is conducive to growth via multiplication.

Following are many of the advantages to this simple and reproducible system of disciple making.

1. LTG's plant the seed, not a seed substitute.

I was once speaking with a very successful church planter who had not only started a church himself, but also had led that church to daughter three others. I asked him, "If you had a plot of land and wanted to grow a farm on it, what would you need to do?" He said, "Well, I'd first plow the field and make sure the soil is good. Then I'd add fertilizer and make sure the land got plenty of sunlight. Finally, I would make sure that the field had plenty of water." I asked him, "Then what?" "I'd cultivate the crop, and take out any weeds." "Then what?" "Well I guess I'd just wait until it was time to harvest." Then I said to him, "All you've got so far is a pile of wet dirt." Then it hit him, "Oh, I'd have to plant the seed!"

Unintentionally, this young pastor had demonstrated the very mistake that the Western church is making—we are doing everything but planting the seed. We need to have the same "aha" experience that he went through.

Jesus made it clear that the seed is the word of God. In the parable of the sower, Jesus tells us, "The sower went out to sow his seed ... and (some) seed fell into the good ground, and grew up, and produced a crop a hundred times as great. ... Now the parable is this: the seed is the word of God (Luke 8:5, 8, 11)."

Peter adds, "For you have been born again not of seed that is perishable but imperishable, that is, through the living and abiding word of God (1 Peter 1:23)."

We are the most biblically privileged generation in all of human history! We have more Bible translations, helpful study tools and mountains of scholarly information than any previous generation in all of human history. Nevertheless, we are also the most biblically illiterate generation this nation has ever seen. In other parts of the world and in other times, people willingly gave their lives for free access to God's word, yet here in the Western world many of us have several unread volumes in a variety of translations collecting dust on the shelf.

No one exposes our shameful lack of Biblical knowledge more accurately and pointedly than pollster and author George Barna. Barna reveals that ...

- 82% of Americans believe that the phrase "God helps those who help themselves" is in the Bible. It isn't.

- 52% thought that the Book of Jonah was not in the Bible. It is.

- 52% believed that Jesus committed sins.

- 58% do not know that Jesus Christ preached the Sermon on the Mount. In all fairness, He was the one who was most selected, but Billy Graham came in a close second and is catching up each year that the survey is conducted!

- 48% think that the Book of Thomas is in the Bible. What's really scary is that 12% of them indicate that they are actually reading the Book of Thomas in their Bibles!

- 12% (25 million Americans) actually believed that Noah's wife was Joan of Arc.[22]

In reading the book of Acts it becomes clear that the word of God itself fueled the growth and expansion of the church.

To gain a perspective of the power of the word in spontaneous church expansion, let's start in Luke's account of the church multiplication movement in Asia Minor and take a brief walk backwards through the book to track the spread of the church to that point. You will see how the word of God is the fire that ignites a new life and passion and which spreads that new life in Christ like a wildfire until ultimately an entire empire is overcome.

Acts 19:20	So **the word** of the Lord was growing mightily and prevailing (in Asia Minor).
Acts 19:10	And this took place for two years, so that all who lived in Asia heard **the word** of the Lord, both Jews and Greeks.
Acts 18:11	And he settled there (Corinth) a year and six months, teaching **the word** of God among them.
Acts 13:49	And **the word** of the Lord was being spread through the whole region (Pisidian Antioch).
Acts 12:24	But **the word** of the Lord continued to grow and to be multiplied.
Acts 8:4	Therefore, those who had been scattered went about preaching **the word**.
Acts 6:7	And **the word** of God kept on spreading; and the number of the disciples continued to increase greatly in Jerusalem, and a great many of the priests were becoming obedient to the faith.

Given this view of the expansion of the church and the power of God's word we can certainly understand why the apostles would conclude, "It is not desirable for us to neglect **the word** of God (Acts 6:2)." Instead of being distracted from the essential ministry of spreading God's word among the growing disciples, they determined, "But we will devote ourselves to prayer, and to the ministry of **the word** (Acts 6:4)."

Unfortunately, today's Western church has allowed herself to be distracted from this vital ministry. It's time for Christian leaders in the western church to make the same determination that these apostles made. Not that we need to lock ourselves up for even longer time in the study preparing for our sermons, but rather be fed by a steady and voluminous intake of Scripture with no purpose other than to hear from God and obey His voice!

The two contributions Martin Luther wanted to make most to Christendom were a Bible that all could read and understand, and a hymnal from which they could sing. He said, "Let them loose. The flame will spread on its own." The flame spread in the early history of the church and has done so throughout history. It can do so once again if we will trust it and let it loose.

To see revival spread through our churches and touch our society we need to trust God's word more than all our "helpful" study tools and great growth ideas. In a sense we need to get out of the way and let God do what He does best, which is the next advantage of the LTG.

2. LTG's remove the middleman

The lay Christian has become totally dependent on clergy to tell him or her what the Bible says and what it means by what it says. Many of the Christians in this country feel they are unable to read the Bible without some professional help. For most, the only time they receive any of the word at all is in sermons at church services.

If you doubt this claim, simply examine the facts. A majority of churchgoers are incapable of reading and understanding the Bibles they own. What is the most published Bible in America today? The King James Version (KJV) by a mile! What is the most read Bible in America today? Again the KJV by a landslide! Here's the problem: According to the US Dept. of Education only 51% of Americans are functionally literate. That means that about half of the people in the United States do not have the literacy levels to comprehend the KJV. According to Barna, three out of four American adults cannot read the Bible they have at home![23] No wonder they are dependent on the clergy for understanding God's word.

Pastors also contribute to the gap between Christians and God's word. Without meaning to, pastors can communicate the importance of needing the help of clergy to understand God's word.

When pastors speak about the Greek or Hebrew meaning of the text, they separate their flock a little further from God's word. After all, how can common Christians understand the Scriptures themselves if they don't know the original languages? The languages are best kept in the pastor's study or the classroom and not in the pulpit.

When a pastor publicly ridicules someone's misinterpretation of Scripture he scares the congregation into thinking that they had better not risk trying to understand it themselves without "professional" help.

Those of us in pastoral ministry have unintentionally programmed our church members to believe that they can't understand the Scriptures without the help of the clergy. By doing so, we have erected a "false priesthood" between the Christian and God's Word. Because we don't trust common Christians to understand the Bible, they don't believe they can.

A young pastor once challenged me regarding the LTG system. He didn't feel I was being responsible allowing people to read the Bible without first giving them a sound "hermeneutic". "Hermeneutic" is a ten-dollar theological term that means the ability to rightly interpret the Bible. He thought it dangerous to actually put the Bible into the hands of ordinary Christians without first giving them training in how to study it. To do otherwise, he felt, was to allow wrong interpretations and spur heresy in the church. I was tempted to suggest that what he really meant was that it allowed interpretations that differed from his own point of view, but restraint got the better of me.

I said, "Our hermeneutic is actually a man-made system we have developed to help us understand the word of God, correct?" He said, "Yes, we need it because we are all sinful, depraved and incapable of understanding the truth of God's word without help." I agreed and emphasized, "We do need help, but we disagree on the best help. You believe that we need help from our hermeneutical systems and I believe that we need help from the author and illuminator of the book—the Holy Spirit." I then asked, "Do you mean to tell me that given a choice of trusting a man-made system or trusting the Holy Spirit, the pure resident author of the Scripture, to interpret the Bible, you would choose the system made by the corrupt and depraved man rather than trusting God? You would rather choose to trust the corrupt man and his system more than the divine author Himself?" He paused a long time before he responded. In fact he didn't really answer my question, he simply said, "You know, I hate to admit it, and I'll deny it if you ask me later, but, you're actually a more pure Biblicist than I am." That was one of the greatest compliments I've ever received.

Am I saying that we don't need a proper hermeneutic to understand Scriptures? Do I mean to say that to use one is to lack faith? No, absolutely not. I strive to apply proper principles of interpretation when I am studying the Bible, and I do teach them to those I train in ministry. The key is in the timing of such training. I train proper interpretation techniques to those who are responsible for teaching others. However, before they ever get to that point in leadership training, they have already been reading and hearing from God in His Scripture for a long time through LTG's. It is when we are responsible for teaching the Bible to others that our hermeneutic becomes most important. I have found that teaching principles of hermeneutics to people who have already learned to read Scripture and to understand the Holy Spirit's illumination in their personal lives becomes very easy. Most find the principles to have already been adapted in their study because they reflect common sense and the Holy Spirit has already helped them along in the process.

One very liberating idea is that we don't have to be responsible to accurately interpret every line and every word in order to read the Bible and gain appropriate truth for life application. I confess that there have been many times that I have read portions of the Bible and found more questions than answers—but that doesn't make the Bible wrong or me irresponsible. It simply means that I still have many levels of depths to plummet into the riches of His word. But I also want to point out that many of those times where I came away with questions I also found relevant truth that spoke to me personally. I have also found that years later, when I pour over old copies of Bibles that have worn out, many of the questions now have answers—but I have also found a whole new set of questions as well! All this shows me that I am a learner and I want to be a learner for the rest of my life! An early church father once claimed that the Bible was shallow enough for a babe to wade in without fear of drowning yet deep enough for theologians to dive into without ever touching the bottom. Who can actually claim that whenever they read the Bible they have full understanding of all that is in it? Who has a monopoly of what real truth and doctrine is? This kind of attitude leads to an arrogant mockery of real Christianity.

As it is, however, we have placed a middleman between the Christian and God's word at every front. For instance, often we hear the gospel first through a tract. After we receive Christ, we are given a fill-in-the-blank booklet to tell us what the Bible says about our new life. We buy a study Bible to interpret for us what the Bible is trying to tell us. Even in theological training we often read more books about the Bible than we do the Bible itself. Instead of digesting God's pure word, we end up taking in predigested spiritual food coming through another's mind and mouth. Predigested food may still have nutrients in it and may be necessary at times, but it isn't much fun to eat. I believe that one of the reasons more people don't read the Bible is that they don't think they will enjoy it. They think of the predigested stuff they've had and expect the Bible to taste the same, but it doesn't! There is nothing in the world like hearing the God of the universe speak to you about your own life and circumstances.

In Hebrews, the writer referred to the recipients as babes who ought to be eating solid food but could only handle milk like a baby (Heb. 5:11-14).

There are a variety of explanations as to what the author meant by milk and what solid food is. While he may have had deeper teachings in mind, I do believe that you can make a case for eating the word directly rather than being dependent upon others' teachings. After all, what is milk but predigested food from another? The mother ingests the food, and it is processed and finally delivered to babes who are absolutely dependent upon their parent for sustenance. The exhortation given is that they ought to have become teachers by now (milk distributors) but rather still had to receive milk from others. All the tools and helps are good, but we also need to hear from God directly without a middleman.

Please don't misunderstand me; I am not advocating that we have ignorance in the pulpit, or in the people of God. In fact, I am suggesting the opposite. The problem is that in spite of our efforts to educate Christians with these tools and teachings we have failed. The people of God do not know the word of God. I believe that the problem is that we have been teaching them what to think instead of how to think. We must remove the barriers between God's word and God's people and see what happens when the two mix. I had a professor in seminary who once told me, "Where the word of God is not known the work of God is not seen."

There was a time when the Scripture was only available to the elite clergy who were literate in the sacred languages. We call that time the *dark ages*! It is time for a new reformation in the Church, an enlightenment with the truth of God's word!

By introducing a middleman to the disciple-making process we have introduced a seed substitute which harms all the succeeding generations. The seed substitute looks like the real thing, boasts of being the real thing, but in fact it ends up confusing the disciples. A synthetic seed is not the same as the real thing. Like the parable of the hormone disrupters we unintentionally sterilize the second generation and though they may appear to be healthy, they are incapable of reproducing.

When one makes a photocopy from another photocopy the quality is slightly reduced. When one makes a fourth generation copy the quality degenerates even more. With each succeeding generation the product becomes more and more corrupted until eventually it is more unlike the original than like it. Every new copy of a previous copy contains all the flaws of all the generations before it as well as its own unique blemishes. The solution is to make all your copies directly from the master itself. This will reduce almost all of the corruption and assure a copy most like the master. The best that a photocopy can be is very much like the original—but there is only one original.

When it comes to reproducing disciples and leaders, the same principles apply. Each succeeding generation must be directly linked to the Master if it is to maintain and reflect the purity and beauty of the Lord. Every generation that only mimics a copy of the Master will reflect back the flaws of both generations. Jesus said that a student can't be better than his teacher but at best he can be like his teacher (Matt. 10:24-25). If the teacher is always the next generation down the chain, then the quality of students and teachers diminishes with each generation. But if the student can learn to have the Lord as his or her teacher, then the quality of disciples will remain high. In fact, with this scenario, a disciple can actually emerge to have a greater extent of influence than his human teacher does if he is pursuing the Lord as his master.

Paul understood that the men he was training must have the Lord Jesus Christ as their ultimate Master. By getting his disciples into the word, and getting the word into his disciples, Paul empowered them to become disciples of the Lord directly, and not just followers of Paul. They must reflect Christ's beauty, purity and design in their own unique lives. Paul was only a copy of the Master; they needed to be directly connected to the Original Himself. In his farewell address to the Asian elders at Ephesus, Paul reminded them of this important truth. He said, "And now I commend you to God and to the word of His grace, which is able to build you up and to give you the inheritance among all those who are sanctified" (Acts 20:32). Thus, when they reached out to others, they in turn could do the same.

If a disciple learns to live his life a certain way just to please the one with whom he is apprenticing, his Christian life will not reflect the power of the Lord, nor will it last through the long haul. If he does reproduce himself in other disciples, they will not only have their own weaknesses, but will reflect the weaknesses of the two previous generations as well.

In spite of his efforts to connect his disciples to the Master Himself, Paul still had some that eventually fell away from the Lord. Phygelus, Hermogenes, both Asians and probably present for Paul's farewell charge in Acts 20, turned away from Paul and took considerable numbers with them (2 Tim. 1:15). Demas, and even Crescens and Titus, may have deserted Paul and compromised their calling (2 Tim. 4:10). Even the Lord Himself lost Judas, so it is inevitable that we will all be disappointed by some of our disciples.

The number who will disappoint us can be dramatically reduced if we can connect them directly to the Master Himself. The connection is found in being accountable to God Himself, and to look "to the word of His grace" which is able to strengthen us in our sanctification (John 17:17). In a sense, the word of God is our master document revealing the character and works of God that we are to copy in our own character and behavior. If we each have as our highest goal to be found pleasing to our Lord, then we will live righteously even when there is no one else around to observe us, save God Himself. This is the only motivation that will keep one in the race to the finish (2 Tim. 4:1-8)!

3. LTG's integrate evangelism with the spiritual formation process.

We have committed an illegitimate divorce! When we separate "evangelism" from "discipleship" we are separating that which God has joined together!

My friend, Stan Leach, director of church planting for the Friends Southwest, describes evangelism and discipleship as two wings of the same plane. You can't fly without both. When they are separated we are destined to crash and burn.

Salvation is a lifelong process. It doesn't begin at Law One and end with a prayer after Law Four! I like the children's fantasy film *The Never Ending Story*. After the film, just before the credits begin to role, instead of saying "The End" it says "The Beginning." The adventure has just begun! They just released *The Never Ending Story Part Four*, so I guess we can take them at their word. Like marriage, when you say your vows, the engagement is over, but the marriage has just begun! When you say the prayer to commit to Jesus, it's not the culmination of your salvation—it's the beginning!

The gospel is not just for the unbeliever, but the Christian. It's the power of God for salvation *for those who believe* (Rom. 1:16, emphasis added). In fact I don't think the non-Christian will take the cross seriously for him or herself until we take it seriously for ourselves! It's not enough that we have once tasted the blessing of the cross. To attract the lost to Jesus we need to have an appetite for the gospel ourselves. The more it means to us, the more attractive it will be to the lost. Why should they be interested in that to which we give feigned interest in ourselves? If they don't see that we need it ourselves, then why would they feel compelled to need it themselves?

Salvation is so much more than mere fire insurance, or reservations made in heaven. Salvation is a transformed life. Salvation is a becoming. Regeneration is an ongoing process of the Holy Spirit in our lives. Each of us should be more like Christ this year than we were the year before. Our lives should reflect more of the grace and truth found in Christ next year than they do this year.

I have as much or more need to take up my cross and follow Jesus today than I did years ago when I first started on this path. My need for freedom remains. My need for being cleansed and renewed is as strong or stronger than ever before. I once heard Billy Graham, who has walked with God much longer than I, say, "The closer I get to heaven the more aware of hell I become."

Theologians refer to this ongoing salvation process as sanctification. It means to be set apart for significance. The idea is that we are in a process of becoming closer to who we are to be in heaven—closer to being like Christ Himself. If we are truly moving closer to God, nearer to holiness, then our awareness of our own flesh must become more obvious to us. Our sensitivity to sin and its subtleties should increase as we grow closer to Christ.

In fact, there is a paradox in the salvation process. We may think that as we grow closer to Christ's likeness, sin decreases and our need for the gospel also decreases, but that assumption is wrong. While it may be true that our life of obedience sees actual acts of sin on the decrease, at the same time we should become more aware of sin and the grip it has had on our lives. We should thus develop a more dependent attitude toward our Savior, His sacrifice and His ongoing ministry in our lives.

It is interesting to see Paul's self-awareness change over time. In his earlier writings he refers to himself as equal to the most eminent of apostles (2 Cor. 12:11). Later, he writes that he is least of the saints (Eph. 3:8). In one of his last writings he calls himself the foremost of all sinners (1 Tim. 1:15). Was his sin and disobedience actually increasing over that time? Of course not. He was getting closer to His Lord and thus becoming more aware of his own weaknesses in the light of Jesus' perfection. He knew his need for the gospel better at the end of his life than he did at the beginning.

We must recognize that salvation is more than a decision made at the end of the sawdust aisle in a tent. Salvation is a process. It is a state of being. It is also a destination. It is so much more than what is sold to people from most pulpits, tracts and crusades today.

There is a strategic place for large evangelistic crusades. They have always been used by the Lord and will continue to be. But they are not sufficient alone to transform lives and fuel a revival. Crusades and stadium events such as Promise Keepers appeal to the people to decide to follow Christ but, as I have argued, that is only the first step in a lifelong process of salvation.

John Wesley used to preach to crowds of up to twenty thousand people outdoors in a day when the only public address system was vocal cords and a good set of lungs. He would preach the gospel with great effectiveness. People would weep and wail over their sin and need of salvation.

Wesley, however, did not rely upon these crusades as the means for lost people to be saved. Rather, he considered the public preaching ministry as merely a means to partially awaken the people to their need of salvation, but would then gather the people into small groups of people where they encountered holiness in accountability. Here, in the class meetings is where Wesley believed that souls were justified before God. He believed this so strongly in fact, that he felt to preach the gospel without forming class meetings was actually detrimental.

He said, "Preach in as many places as you can. Start as many classes as you can. Do not preach without starting new classes."[24] In his book, *To Spread the Power: Church Growth in the Wesleyan Spirit*, George Hunter says,

> (Wesley) observed that awakening people without folding them into redemptive cells does more harm than good! In a journal entry of 1743 he declares, "The devil himself desires nothing more than this, that the people of any place should be half-awakened and then left to themselves to fall asleep again. Therefore, I determine by the grace of God not to strike one stroke in any place where I cannot follow the blow."[25]

Wesley brought together the key ingredients of life transformation into close relationships of accountability, which were not dependent upon highly trained leaders. The class meetings multiplied and kept pace with the large evangelistic preaching ministry. The system was so effective that more people came to Christ and joined the church and more churches were started after his death than while he was alive. His influence lived well beyond his life span and still exists today.

Perhaps we do damage by awakening people to their sin only to leave them unaccounted for. They go back to their lives as they were only a little more hardened to the gospel having "tried it once" and finding it ineffective. This helps to explain the pitiful results that crusade evangelism has in church attendance in any given area.

Because we have cheapened the salvation process, and thus the gospel, we see pitiful results to our own evangelistic efforts. According to Barna, the majority of people who make a decision for Christ are no longer in the church just eight weeks later.[26] This is partly because we have not understood what salvation truly is and thus we short sell the meaning and power of the gospel. If nonbelievers see its relevance and power in our own lives they will want it too. They must see it in us before they will be willing to hear it from us. Donald Soper has said, "Christianity must mean everything to us before it will mean anything to others."[27]

I like what Francis of Assisi said: "Preach the gospel at all times, and if necessary use words."

As it stands currently, the common Christian is far from integrating the gospel and evangelism into their spiritual development.

- 40% of born-again Christians, according to the Barna Research Group, do not have a clue what the word "gospel" means.

- 53% did not know what "John 3:16" means. One comedy film about NBA basketball had a wild fan point to a banner which read "John 3:16" and yelled to the coach, "Hey John, that's not a Bible verse, that's your road record!" That's about the level of understanding today!

- 81% (4:5) of born-again Christians do not know what the phrase "Great Commission" means. They think its something like 25% of the profits![28]

The LTG system incorporates evangelism with spiritual formation. There is a subtle yet effective strategy inherent within the system itself. Being a real testimony to the greatness of Jesus is a part of one's character formation and is included in the accountability questions (number 1). It isn't as necessary to explain all four spiritual laws each week as it is to be a living and verbal testimony of love and appreciation for Jesus with your life. We have found that when this happens, seeds are scattered in relationship that will often sprout into fuller and deeper discussions at a later and more appropriate time. It produces a more natural, relational evangelism that flows out of one's personal redemptive experience. Not forced, but not subdued either, it is a spontaneous expression of love that comes from the joy of salvation itself.

Often Christian leaders have thought that if we train our people in methods of evangelism they will automatically have more courage to share their faith with others. We assumed that it is training that is needed, but we have found that training does not overcome the barriers that keep Christians from sharing the gospel. Offering more and better training is a good thing, but we have found that it does not necessarily produce more evangelists in the church or the world.

What I have found with the LTG system is that people share the gospel because it is a part of spiritual growth—a natural expression of a soul that is being touched by God. When people become connected to God by the Holy Spirit, they become witnesses (Acts 1:8). Later, I have had people come and ask me for training in evangelism so that they can be more effective with the contacts they have already made just by being a living testimony. People who ask for training in evangelism because they have a friend whom they love and are praying for and who is asking them good questions make the best students. They come to the table as eager learners motivated to receive and apply all that is taught.

Add to the process daily intercession for the souls of lost people and the burden for the gospel becomes a natural product of a growing disciple. It is interesting that the very men Jesus instructed to pray for the harvest (Matt. 9:37, 38) are the ones He sent into the fields in the next chapter (Matt 10:5). Praying for lost people cultivates an authentic compassion for them.

The gospel flies best on the internal motivation of a life that has been touched by God rather than any external pressure from methodology or persuasive tactics.

Some people in my LTG's don't even realize that others are embarrassed about bringing Christ up in conversation. They see their witness as a part of their spiritual life and growth rather than an obligation they grudgingly take upon themselves. The gospel means so much to them that they can't help but share the good news with others! Can it be that a big part of our hesitancy to witness is a learned behavior? Can it be that a Spirit-filled life will produce a bold witness in the lives of Christians (Acts 1:8)? All through the book of Acts, one thing is clear—Spirit-filling resulted in bold witnessing. I have to admit that I was quite surprised by how easily people responded to the challenge to be a testimony of Christ in their world. In fact, it is not rare for a group to go for several weeks with unanimous affirmation to the question, "Have you been a testimony this week to the greatness of Jesus Christ with both your words and actions?"

4. LTG's form life-long spiritual disciplines.

The disciplines introduced in an LTG, reading Scripture, confessing sin, and praying for lost people, are sadly lacking in the Western church today. These can become the foundation upon which other spiritual disciplines can be built.

Americans are not a people used to saying "no" too much. We usually expect instant gratification. The ideas of discipline and delayed gratification are not valued much. An LTG can introduce a new disciple to the value of discipline and he or she will be more receptive to trying other spiritual disciplines once they recognize their benefits.

5. LTG's allow the Holy Spirit His rightful place in spiritual formation.

Kevin, who was part owner in a plumbing business, was a good man. He was an elder in our church. He was faithful, available and an example of what an elder should be. I never really considered having Kevin in an LTG because in my mind he was already walking with God. After seeing so many lives changed through the LTG system, a godly jealousy was aroused in some of the elders in my church, including Kevin. I began meeting with two of these men. Kevin took quickly to the disciplines and began to grow immediately.

We were reading the book of Revelation at the time, and I was teaching a series on the role of the Holy Spirit in the Christian's life when something new began to happen in Kevin. It was Good Friday and Kevin had been fasting when he was called to a job site on the other side of town. On the way there he felt the conviction of the Holy Spirit. He turned off the radio and the Lord laid upon his heart that Jesus died on the cross for his sin. This was not any new idea for Kevin, but that day, the Spirit made it clear to him what price Jesus had to pay for his salvation. Kevin could barely contain the emotional outpouring that came upon him.

That Sunday, Easter, Kevin was giving our announcements in church. Kevin was not a tremendous speaker by any means, but he had a warm and friendly personality so we often had him greet the congregation on Sundays with announcements. This particular Sunday it seemed as though a different man stood up to speak. He said, "Any important announcements can be found in your bulletins, but turn in your Bibles to Revelation chapter four." Kevin went on to share some thoughts on the glory of heaven and the worship of

Jesus When he was finished, there was hardly a dry eye in the auditorium. We concluded that there were two possibilities, either God had done a new work in his heart, or he had been secretly abducted by aliens and replaced by this imposter.

I began to encourage Kevin's newfound giftedness with more opportunities and he began to grow in his abilities. A short time later, while in transit to another job site, Kevin heard clearly from the Lord a call to preach and teach God's word. In just a little over a year, Kevin was given his first pastorate. He took the lead of our church as I was called to start a new work. Our church had made Kevin an elder, but the Holy Spirit had made him a pastor.

From plumber to pastor in a little over a year, Kevin is evidence of what the Holy Spirit can do in a life that is empowered with the word and a relationship of accountability. It is important to note that the Holy Spirit is by no means finished with Kevin. He continues to grow and still has much to learn. It is not how much stuff Kevin has learned that qualifies him, but that he is called, learning and is still listening to the Lord.

The Holy Spirit is a surprisingly good teacher! The LTG's allow the Spirit of God and the Word of God to take their rightful place in leading the Christian into all truth. Most segments of the Christian faith believe in the illumination ministry of the Holy Spirit. However, many do not trust in it. When it comes to understanding the Bible, we tend to trust more in our interpretive systems and apologetic reasoning than we do in the author Himself. Many churches have been going on for far too long without the help of their most powerful and influential member—the Holy Spirit! He is, without a doubt, the best convictor of sin (John 16:8-11); witness for Jesus (John 15:26-27); worshiper of Christ (John 16:14); and teacher of Scripture (John 14:26; 16:13-15) in your church! He is named the "One called alongside to help" (John 14:16-17). We could all use His help!

In the book *Pastors at Risk,* Jerry Bridges says,

> One way to gauge ministry is to ask yourself, 'If the Holy Spirit were to back out of this effort, would it collapse?' Many ministries would continue because they are humanly produced programs.[29]

When Paul was giving his farewell address to the elders in Ephesus, he acknowledged that it is the Holy Spirit who calls out His leaders for the work He desires of them. He said, "Be on guard for yourselves and for all the flock, among which the Holy Spirit has made you overseers, to shepherd the church of God which He purchased with His own blood (Acts 20:29)." It was the Holy Spirit that called out Paul and Barnabas to take the gospel to the Gentiles (Acts 13:1-3).

Because the LTG system is leaderless and uses only the word of God rather than a man-made curriculum, the Holy Spirit is given greater opportunity to lead, guide and call out the disciples into the ministries He has for them.

6. LTG's empower common Christians to obey the Great Commission for the rest of their lives!

The Great Commission given by Jesus is a command to take the gospel to all the nations and make disciples. It is found in each of the four gospels (Matt. 28:18-20; Mark 16: Luke 24:; John 20:) as well as the book of Acts (1:8). The last word Jesus gave to His disciples in person before He ascended to heaven was this command. It is called the Great Commission because of its emphasis, its all encompassing authority as well as its global boundaries. It is the divine purpose handed down to the church from Jesus Himself with all authority of heaven and earth behind it.

Unfortunately the actual percentage of Christians who are fulfilling the commission is quite low. As someone has said, "There is one thing that Christians and non-Christians share in common—they both hate evangelism!" Called by some, the "Great Omission" few Christians are actually being empowered to fulfill this calling. Not that they haven't been given the power to do so, but they are just not naturally accessing the power that has been granted to them.

Because of its simplicity, after only a brief exposure to this system, Christians (no matter how long they have believed) are equipped to make disciples for the rest of their lives. This is a means to release the whole church into the fulfillment of the Great Commission. The potential consequence of laity that is empowered and motivated to make more and better disciples of all the nations is staggering! We don't have to wait for leaders to be trained or complicated methods to be passed along. A new believer can be released to pass on the baton in just weeks rather than years. The possibility of fulfilling the Great Commission in this generation is indeed a reality!

The command given by Jesus in Matthew 28 to "Go and make disciples" is in the present tense, indicating a continual mandate. In my years of ministry, I have not found any method that produces such powerful results in fulfilling the Great Commission. I personally plan on using this system for the rest of my life to make as many disciples of the kingdom as I can before Christ calls me home!

7. LTG's mobilize lay people for ministry.

When Christians confess their sin to one another every week, and read large passages of Scripture repeatedly, they begin to have a change of heart. Soon grudging duty is replaced by an internal drive to serve out of a love for Christ and others.

Once they feel empowered to do the most significant ministry of all—making disciples—common Christians actually feel prepared and equipped "to do *every* good work" (2 Timothy 2:22; 3:17, emphasis added)! Their own life-change becomes a spring of life and ministry flowing into the lives of others (John 7:37-39).

8. LTG's provide tangible evidence of an emerging leader

The crying need of the church today is for leadership. From workers in the nursery to missionaries sent overseas, the church is lacking leaders. The need is for more leaders and better leaders. Jesus Himself identified the need for workers as the one limiting factor in reaching the harvest (Matt. 9:37). His solution was to pray and ask the Lord of the harvest to raise up workers from the harvest for the harvest.

While the LTG system does not produce leaders in and of itself, it does provide a deep well in which to discover emerging leaders.

The LTG's provide the perfect initial testing grounds for emerging leadership. If a person can't influence and multiply a group of two, why should we entrust him or her with 15? With 50? Or a church of 200, or more?

When anyone approaches me desiring to lead a ministry I always challenge him or her to first initiate and multiply an LTG. This helps in several ways:

1. It tests the real fortitude of the potential leader. I can see whether or not he can be obedient to the most basic of commands.

2. I can have confidence that my leadership team are in vital relationships of accountability and are reading the word of God regularly. And, yet, I don't have to be the one looking over their shoulders to make sure they are taking care of business in their personal lives.

3. This also provides me with an opportunity to see if leadership candidates can be faithful before I entrust them with weightier responsibilities.

4. Another advantage to starting the process of leadership development at the disciple-making level is that I am assured that those who actually emerge as leaders do indeed know how to make and multiply disciples. This is a skill which, unfortunately, has been sadly lacking in Christian leadership of recent years. Most of us have heard stories of people who have gone through years of seminary training; raised prayer and financial support; arranged for passports and visas; learned another language; relocated their family to another part of the globe to live in another culture, only to discover that they do not know how to make and multiply disciples—*in any language*! There is no other word for such but foolishness! This has to stop. Paul wrote to Timothy regarding the appointment of deacons, "Let them first be tested, then let them serve as deacons."

5. As leaders reproduce themselves, a natural benefit is more leaders. Like produces like. We tend to reproduce after our own kind. Of course, as I reinvest those new leaders right back into the Great Commission the payoff promises to be great!

9. LTG's release the cell leader and pastor for more focused ministry.

Though the evangelical church seems to be taking strategic steps toward a cell-based ministry, we must go further at lowering the bar of ministry beyond the cell leader to every Christian. Too much is still placed on the shoulders of the cell leader. He or she must simultaneously minister to a seeker, a person with a broken marriage, and answer another's theological questions. Meanwhile another wants to do an in-depth study of the end times and the book of Revelation and yet another wants to reach out to others in evangelism. With all this on the shoulders of a lay leader, we thrust on top of it the need to train up a new leader and bring this diverse group to a point of multiplication within a year! Most trained pastors and missionaries are not sufficiently equipped to be able to do all of this.

The LTG does provide much-needed help for the cell leader, and releases him or her to focus leadership on a specific task with motivated and growing disciples.

Many of the New Testament "one anothers" are functioning at the LTG level, which releases the cell leader and pastor from being the chief caregiver.

People feel connected, cared for and helped by one another; so there is less demand on the pastor to fill this need. The pastor can concentrate on equipping leaders, while "the whole body, being fitted and held together by that which every joint supplies, according to the proper working of each individual part, causes the growth of the body for the building up of itself in love (Eph. 4:11-16 NAS)."

10. LTG's tap the internal motivation of the disciples.

This system of disciple-making works because it is driven by an internal motivation. It stimulates a hunger within. The Lord Himself promised that when we hunger for righteousness we would find satisfaction (Matt. 5:6). The Life Transformation Groups continue because the people in them want them to.

LTG's utilize a form of sanctified peer pressure. We all know from experience that peer pressure can motivate more than threat or outward compulsion. Peer pressure exists because of an intrinsic desire to be liked and accepted. The Life Transformation Groups pull people together and push them forward in their growth because the people within them want to grow and want to grow together.

It has been my experience that the longer people are involved in the LTG system the more they value it. Often the leader of a discipleship curriculum gets bored with the material after two or three rounds. With the LTG's, the disciples do not get bored, for one can hardly exhaust the word of God.

Another way that the LTG system taps internal motivation is through the personal accountability questions. Ordinarily, we find it most uncomfortable to bring up problem areas in another's life. Few are comfortable with confrontation. Those who are, are uncomfortable to be around. Even in close relationships in which there is warmth and acceptance it is still difficult to bring up a potential weakness, thinking that we are prying into an area that is none of our business. All kinds of doubts flood our minds. "What if I offend him? What if he doesn't want to talk about it? I could lose our friendship if I bring this up. Who am I to judge my brother anyway?"

It is so much easier to talk about our struggles when we bring them up ourselves. In the LTG system the accountability works both ways. The burden of confrontation is removed because it is the questions that bring out the struggles. Because the questions raise the personal issues, all involved feel a greater freedom to support, help and even challenge one another. The questions are for each person in the group, and because all are sharing personal struggles, the group becomes a safe place for transparency and vulnerability.

11. LTG's release spontaneous multiplication into the church at the grass-roots level.

Early in the development of this system I was teaching that the groups need to multiply. I believed that I needed to stress this point or the groups would not reproduce. I applied a lot of external pressure and persuasion to try and get the groups to multiply.

At the same time, I had been studying spontaneous multiplication principles from the word of God and some other books. Some ladies in my church challenged me one evening by saying, "Don't talk to us about multiplication. We don't want to hear it. We like our group and don't want to split up." I considered this a good opportunity to test the natural function of planting seeds in good soil, so I told them that if they didn't want to multiply they didn't have to. I intentionally stopped pushing reproduction to test the truth of natural and spontaneous multiplication. Within about four months, that same group of women became three groups without any help from me.

In the past, I found that I needed to sweat and bleed to see even the most modest multiplication occur in discipleship. Today, I have seen the kind of spontaneous multiplication that I have always longed for but was doubting I would ever experience. We need to remember that reproduction is a natural function of the church and that it's part of God's design and plan. The power to produce multiplication is already inherent in the body of Christ; we need only to tap that power. If we would only plant the seed, rather than a seed substitute, into soil that is prepared, we would see multiplication.

The very fact that it takes so much personal effort to see the most measly results in reproduction of disciples is strong evidence that we are doing something wrong, something that is not natural to the process.

Jesus described, through parables, a kingdom that didn't have any trouble expanding and multiplying. Luke documents a movement that gained such momentum through spontaneous multiplication of disciples and churches that its opponents accused Paul of turning the world upside down! We may have read of such a thing happening in church history or on foreign mission fields, but most of us must confess that we have never experienced such spontaneous multiplication in the western church.

If we focus on making disciples, and keep the system simple and solid, multiplication becomes easy and natural. The thought of multiplication becomes more palatable in the disciples. Once the disciples experience a taste of reproduction, it is embraced more readily in other levels of church ministry. Multiplication of cells, ministries and even churches will be a more natural function because multiplication is in the genetic code of the base unit of the church—the disciples.

As was mentioned before, there is not a single command to plant a church or to multiply small groups. There is a lot of church planting and multiplying of groups going on in the New Testament, but not because the church was instructed to do so. The reason that groups and churches multiplied is because the first generation of Christians were obeying a very specific and simple command—to make disciples! When Christians are obedient to this single command, it results in the multiplying of groups and churches. To attempt to multiply groups and churches without multiplying disciples is not only disobedient, but it is downright impossible!

Many are very intentional about multiplying groups and churches, assuming that disciple-making will result, but the results are less than effective. This is Biblically backwards! The truth is that only when we become intentional about making and multiplying disciples can we be assured that groups and churches will multiply.

I have seen groups multiply through conversion growth in as little as three months with the LTG system. In fact, multiplication occurred faster and easier than I was prepared for.

The concept of LTG's was first introduced in a leadership development workbook titled *Raising Leaders for the Harvest*,[30] which I co-authored with Bob Logan a little more than a year before this writing. Though the workbook itself has yet to be translated into any other language, currently I have heard of LTG's on almost every continent on the globe!

Recently, while in Australia, I met a man who had been using the strategy. He heard about it from a common friend. He told me of how he had been speaking with another friend who is a church leader on the island of Sri Lanka, south of India, and who had run into frustrations with typical discipleship methodology. The LTG concept was passed on through the phone lines and now LTG's are multiplying on the island of Sri Lanka. Who knows where they will go from there!

The most dramatic example of multiplication I have seen yet occurred in the beginning of my new ministry of planting a church in the greater Long Beach area that reaches young people with a postmodern view of life. I began an LTG on the campus of Long Beach City College with two students. After one month of meeting together we were sitting down in the school cafeteria having coffee and going over the accountability questions. We were on about the second question when another student came by, recognized his friend whom I was meeting with and took an interest in the questions and what we were doing. His friend asked if he wanted to join us but he couldn't meet at this same time, so they set up a time to get together and he went on his way as we moved to question number three.

By the time we got to the fifth question another student happened to come by, see what we were doing and asked if he could be a part of a group as well. The other student I had been meeting with set up a time and place to begin meeting with him.

We went back to the questions and got as far as the sixth question when one of my guys saw someone he hadn't seen in a while so he excused himself for a moment and went to talk with her. When he returned he told us that his friend needed a group and wanted to know who she could meet with. We discussed the possibilities and settled on one girl we thought would be the best person to ask to meet with this girl.

By the time we got to the last question the very girl we had in mind to begin meeting with her came up to us to see what we were doing. After explaining the other girl's need she agreed to try and get together with her.

In one hour a single group multiplied into three other groups, and as usual, yours truly was the one lagging behind! By the next day I also had a new group. Within two weeks we had up to ten groups going on two college campuses and in the community!

These groups spread like a wild fire because the breath of God blows on obedient disciples who find fuel in dry lives longing to burn for the Lord. Because the system is simple enough to pass on with one easy description the flame spreads unhindered. Ordinary Christians are empowered to do the most important work any of us can do.

Chapter 10:
Common Objections to the
LTG System

In the few years that we have been applying these principles and seeing fruit I have had a chance to consider some objections to what I've shared. In this chapter I will share the most common objections and a response to each.

1. They are out of control!

Because the groups give birth, multiply and die spontaneously, it would be very difficult to keep track of them. The temptation in trying to do so would be to control them, which would stifle their potential. My recommendation is to keep track of the numbers in worship attendance and the numbers of ministries and cell groups, but allow these groups to be controlled by the Holy Spirit and none other.

A good question to ask is, "Who was in control of the expansion of the church in the book of Acts?" It is clear from chapter one to chapter twenty-eight that there was not a single human leader in charge of the expansion of the early church. The Holy Spirit was in charge. He is mentioned some 57 times in 28 chapters.

Control is often a big concern in our churches. We take great measures to control our activities for fear that all hell will break loose. I don't think hell is our greatest threat right now. Jesus already dealt with the power of hell, and he has declared that hell's gates pose no barrier to the church's advance.

The real question we need to ask is, "What will we do when all heaven breaks loose in our churches?" Would we be prepared if revival really came? Can we handle the lack of control? Can our egos manage not having the answers? Could we be comfortable with the chaos? Our church structures, our doctrinal statements, our denominational polities and distinctives are insufficient to contain the wealth and the power of heaven. Heaven is beyond our grasp, beyond our comprehension and beyond our control! Perhaps we should count the cost before we pray, "Thy kingdom come, Thy will be done on earth as it is in heaven."

If we are willing to relinquish control and allow for spontaneous multiplication in our churches, we will see the gospel go further than we ever dreamed possible. In the classic book written ahead of its time, *The Spontaneous Expansion of the Church*, Roland Allen describes the advantage of losing control in a release of spontaneous multiplication.

> By spontaneous expansion I mean something which we cannot control. And if we cannot control it, we ought ... to rejoice that we cannot control it. For if we cannot control it, it is because it is too great, not because it is too small for us. The great things of God are beyond our control. Therein lies a vast hope. Spontaneous expansion could fill the continents with the knowledge of Christ: our control cannot reach as far as that. We constantly bewail our limitations: open doors unentered; doors closed to us as foreign missionaries; fields white to the harvest which we cannot reap. Spontaneous expansion could enter open doors, force closed ones, and reap those white fields. Our control cannot: it can only appeal pitifully for more men to maintain control.[31]

2. The questions are too personal to expect new believers to answer.

When people are ready to change they are ready to address the personal problem areas in their lives. Even in the world today, those who don't believe in Jesus are willing to stand before a crowd and confess to being an alcoholic, drug addict or to some other form of compulsive sin behavior dealt with by a twelve-step program. They are willing to do so because they know that it's the only way to be free of the behavior. How much more should we who have the truth, know God personally, and have the Holy Spirit within be willing to openly confess our sins one to another in a safe place?

In my experience, the truth is new believers and even pre-Christians are more receptive to this system than older Christians who have been able to keep people at arm's length over the years by wearing a mask of spirituality.

New believers don't really think that the questions are too personal. They don't even know to think such because they are only just forming their opinion of what this "Christianity stuff" is all about. The questions are too personal for staid Christians who are content with the status quo and threatened by opening up the closet and exposing what is inside.

It is true that the LTG system has a high commitment level for a ground floor entry point to the church. Many, if not most, church growth philosophies today try to lower the level of commitment up front so as to attract more people and hopefully woo them into Christianity gradually. They treat the salvation of people as a step-by-step gradual process, which is true. But it is my belief that we can sometimes sabotage our message by cheapening the strength of the truth we embrace. If it is true, then it should be true at every level and have strength at every level, even the entry point.

I think that the lost of the world will respond well to truth that we embrace wholeheartedly and do not compromise in any way. We are in a day when it is important to call sin, sin and truth, truth! I have found that lost people who want to be saved respond well to authentic lives willing to admit their need for forgiveness and grace. I have found in my experience that those who need their lives changed thrive in a safe place where others are willing to openly confess their own deficiencies. In fact, it is when we hide this authenticity from the world, and pretend to be better than we are, that the world takes offense at our hypocrisy and rejects our message.

When Jesus spoke of an entry point into salvation and the kingdom of God, He didn't attempt to lower the standard so that more could enter in, He did the very opposite. He said,

> If anyone wishes to come after Me let him deny himself, pick up his cross and follow Me. He who wishes to save his life shall lose it, and he who is willing to lose his life for my sake, and for the gospel's sake shall keep it.

This is hardly a "seeker sensitive" approach to winning the unchurched. It doesn't allow for anonymity. It doesn't allow people to slowly come out of the world. It calls for a strong and uncompromising commitment right up front, at the entry level. The LTG challenges people to deny themselves and follow the Savior and people have responded. At the same time, however, it provides the support needed to carry on with the commitment.

3. The amount of suggested reading is too much for a busy person to do.

If an average reader will give half-an-hour every day to reading the Scripture, he or she will be able to keep up with the required amount. Most of us give at least that much time to getting ready each morning for the day ahead. If we can devote that much time to our physical readiness, why not our spiritual? Many people can't get through the day without reading the sports page of the newspaper, or Ann Landers' column, yet we can go a whole week or month without reading God's word. Some of us in the church today are more religious about hearing Leno's monologue than hearing from God through Scripture. No wonder there is no power in some of our churches!

The amount of reading required for an LTG is comparable to watching a half-hour sitcom on TV. Certainly we can afford the time to read God's word because we all give at least that much time to watching the television each night.

I have found that the busier I get, the more I need to read the Scripture! I have recently reached a point in my life where if I don't read the Scripture, I cannot effectively juggle the demands of my life and maintain a level of sanity or composure needed to remain fruitful.

I remember reading that Martin Luther said, "I am so busy that I must spend the first three hours of every day in prayer." I used to admire him for this, and thought that he was an example well beyond my reach. But in recent days I have personally come to understand what he meant. In order to be able to deal with the external pressures of leadership he needed to have an internal strength to balance the demands of life and ministry and maintain a healthy strength to go the distance. That internal strength comes from extended times in devotional prayer and meditation of the Scripture. Like an aircraft that flies at 35,000 feet, the cabin needs to be equalized to handle the pressure and make life comfortable. In the same way, the more we read the Scripture and pray, the better prepared we will be to handle life's external pressures. In fact, if you think you are effective now and are not reading much Scripture, you haven't seen anything yet!

Most of us would be ashamed if we compared the amount of books, magazines and newspaper articles we have poured into our minds with the amount of God's word we have invested into our souls. Doesn't that tell us that we really value the world's philosophies more than God's? This must change if we are ever to become a living example of the people of God! We can start by investing approximately half-an-hour each day to hearing from God!

4. The groups are too legalistic; they'll make the Bible a chore to read.

The truth is that most only read small portions of Scripture as it is, and it is usually a chore to read that much! Many who currently read Scripture regularly do so out of duty not desire. The fact is that Bible reading today is already considered by most to be a chore!

How tragic! I believe that the reason that people consider it a chore is because they haven't fallen in love with it yet. They haven't developed an appetite for it. There is a real sense in which the Scriptures are an acquired taste. Those who love the word of God have found that the more they read it the more they love it.

Have you ever received a love letter in the mail from someone you're crazy about? I can't imagine a man receiving a love letter from someone he truly cared about and setting it on the dresser unopened for a few days. Wouldn't it be strange if he finally opened it and read the first couple lines and said to himself, "Well, that's enough good thoughts for the day," then closed the unfinished letter for another day. This is not the way we read love letters, but unfortunately it is the way we approach the Bible—God's love letter written to us.

The reason that people don't appreciate the word of God yet is because they haven't tasted it enough. Most people take the Bible in small doses of a chapter here and a verse there, and find that it doesn't speak to their life. We take our Bibles like medicine believing that a little bit is good for us and will keep us healthier even though we don't like the way it tastes. It's as though we think that a verse a day keeps the devil away.

Those who read the Scripture in large amounts, in whole context, and repetitively, quickly develop an appetite for it. I have yet to find someone who has been faithful in an LTG that doesn't learn to appreciate the word of God and develop a true hunger for it.

Jesus said, "Man shall not live on bread alone but on every word that proceeds from the mouth of God (Matt. 4:4)." We need to develop a hunger for God's word!

Sure, there are mornings when you open the Bible out of duty rather than desire, but most of those mornings soon become a lively spiritual time because you spend enough time in the word to overcome the complacency and find God speaking to your own life situation. If we were only reading a chapter a day, that would not happen. Once you have heard God speak directly into your life from His Word, you soon begin to want more. Eventually you can develop a godly addiction—much as a dedicated runner does for the endorphins released in a good workout.

I once read of one man who was so consistent in his joyous walk with God that he was asked, "Do you wake up every morning with such joy?" He answered, "No ma'am, I often wake up as a monster and then I read, and I keep reading until I do have this joy."

The first time I saw this appetite for God's word in another's heart was when Marty and I were just beginning our LTG. We were reading Romans twice in a week. Marty read Romans all the way through once and then read it a second time up to chapter 16, verse 24 and intentionally stopped short of reading the last paragraph. When we met together that week I asked him if he finished the reading and he looked at me with a smile and said, "Nope, we get to read it again this week." He intentionally didn't finish the reading just so that he could read it again at least a couple more times (in fact, he did this more than once). He wanted more reading, not less. This was a new hunger that I hadn't seen in disciples previously. Imagine what the church would look like if even twenty percent of our people had this kind of appetite for the word of God.

I was amazed when my fellow disciple, Kevin, would finish reading a whole gospel or Acts in our LTG and read Hebrews on the side during the week! Thirty plus chapters wasn't enough to satisfy his thirst. This is what can happen to people who are willing to invest a half-an-hour each day in reading God's word. People fall in love with the word, and even better, they fall in love with its author as He speaks to them personally and powerfully.

Unfortunately, in most of our churches today we have made the Bible something to be studied or interpreted rather than something to be simply read, admired and obeyed. Some of us are to the point that God can't speak to us through His word without a commentary, a study Bible, an exhaustive concordance and a Bible encyclopedia. For some the Bible is not a love letter anymore but a legal document in which every word and punctuation demands careful research. Imagine what your sweetheart would think if you treated his or her love letter with that kind of scrutiny.

I understand that there is a place for a deeper study of God's word. I am merely adding that there is also a place for reading it for what it truly is— God's word to you personally.

In my experience, it is not unusual to hear people complain in the first week or two of an LTG that they don't get to really study the Scriptures because they are too busy reading them. This complaint only comes from those who have been Christians for a long time and it only comes in the first few weeks. Once they have actually done the level of reading that the LTG suggests, in just a few weeks they realize how much they truly are receiving. The repetition, and the sheer volume, begins to awaken the reader to truth and he or she begins to become acquainted again with the voice of God. In fact, I have found that reading the Scripture in this way actually stimulates further study rather than reduce it. Questions naturally arise from the reading which motivates the reader to find out more. It is not uncommon to have people in an LTG still studying passages from a book in the Bible that was read weeks earlier even though the group has already moved on to another book in its weekly reading.

5. The groups will allow heresy to run rampant in the church!

There is no reason to fear these groups! They pose no threat to the Body, and do better without being policed. If heresy is a concern, these groups, without controls, are ideal! If a bad apple gets in, only two others are potentially infected. There is no room for power-hungry people who want to influence a crowd of believers. This system would not be attractive to such a person.

The fact is that these groups are the best thing you can do to reduce the threat of heresy! Heresies develop when: (a) the congregation is ignorant of truth, not feeding on the word of God, (b) the Scriptures are taken out of context, and (c) controlling individuals want to influence large numbers of naive people. All three of these factors are eliminated with this strategy! Because the believers are reading entire books of the Bible in context, natural checks and balances are inherent within each group. People in the group are less likely to be led astray because they are reading the same Scripture themselves. Not only is each disciple reading the same Scripture in context but is indwelt by the author—the Holy Spirit. Of course there is no way to completely eliminate the threat of heresy, but this is a very effective way to reduce it.

Chapter 11:
Common Questions
to the LTG System

The questions I have most often heard are listed in this chapter and I have done my best to answer them satisfactorily.

1. Can I reduce the reading and still be effective?

We do not recommend that you decrease the suggested reading. In our own field-testing we have discovered that when the reading is reduced, the disciple's growth and the LTG's multiplication is dramatically stunted. In contrast, however, when a group chooses to increase the reading to the amount we have suggested, then Christian growth increases exponentially!

Our youth pastor, Darrell, shared with me one day that the guys in his group were not getting their reading done every week. He was frustrated because they would be reading the same book over and over again and not make any progress. I asked him how much they were reading each week and he looked a little embarrassed and said, "We're only reading about seven to ten chapters a week, and they still can't get the reading done!" I suggested they increase the reading to thirty chapters a week. "What?" he said, "If they can't get ten chapters done in a week, what would make you think that they can do thirty?" I said, "Just try it." As pastor, I guess my authority was enough, or maybe he wanted to prove me wrong; either way, he gave it a try.

About a month later we were meeting for another mentoring appointment and I asked him how his LTG was doing. "Oh," he said, "you'd be amazed! Since I increased the reading assignment they have all finished the reading each week. I don't understand it, but it worked." I told him, "They weren't getting enough of a taste of the word to really enjoy it. They weren't taking the Bible reading that seriously because they weren't challenged to."

There is value in stretching a Christian's capacity for reading rather than keeping them comfortable. If a group is able to complete the assigned reading every week, they will not get all that they could from the reading, because the value of repetition will be removed from the process. We have found that often a group will stay in a specific book long enough for one or more of the members to discover something especially significant. For this reason, when someone has not finished the reading for any given week, we go into the next week expecting to discover what the Holy Spirit has intended for us— something that we may have missed in the previous week(s). To find a good balance with the amount of reading, we suggest that you experiment until you find an amount that keeps the group in the same book for about four weeks before moving on. For most, that is about 25-30 chapters per week.

If a group has a slow reader, or even an illiterate one, we have found that they can keep up with the group simply by acquiring the Bible on audio tape and listening to the assigned amount with the same repetition as the group. We have even had one LTG use the Scripture reading as a means to teach reading skills to an illiterate person. In such a case, however, I recommend that the learner read a small amount to begin with (depending on the extent of illiteracy), and supplement the rest of the reading by listening to tapes. You can increase the actual amount of reading as the learner becomes more proficient. During the meetings, you can teach literacy using the passage that they have been assigned to read and which they have already listened to on tape. This will maintain the integrity of the accountability in the LTG without compromising the literacy training.

NOTE: I highly recommend that the groups read the Scripture dramatically, out loud, as often as possible. This alone will increase their retention threefold! There is evidence that this engages more of the brain because we use so many more muscles. It also increases retention because we have to pay attention if we fluctuate our voices in dramatic fashion. One other reason that the memory is enhanced is that we receive the word through more than just one gateway to the mind. Rather than just using the eye gate, we also hear the words and can tap our kinetic learning as well with dramatic gestures. The word gets in through more than one entry point and finds a more active and alert mind when it gets there. Try this yourself. Of course, you will need to find a lonely place where you will be undistracted and unheard—then again, maybe not.

2. Can I change the accountability questions?

We encourage you to adapt the questions freely to suit the needs of your people. As we have already mentioned, there are certain areas of accountability that I suggest you cover with the accountability questions you develop. One is an opportunity to confess sins. Another is to be some kind of testimony to Christ in the week. The one question that we have included—the one that asks if they have been a testimony to the supremacy of Christ in both their words and actions—subtly yet effectively introduces evangelism into spiritual formation for all disciples. If, for example, you allow a group to remove the verbal element of their testimony from the question, evangelism is taken from the process. By keeping the question unaltered, growing disciples will begin to share with others and actually increase their desire and skill in the art of winning souls. The question doesn't ask that the Christian share the death, burial and resurrection of Christ every week, but that they somehow communicate to others that Jesus is awesome!

There is a subtle yet purposeful design to this strategy. Christians will begin to share with their friends, neighbors and co-workers (albeit softly at first). As the weeks go by, the disciples will desire to go further in evangelism, which is often prompted by the seeker's questions and prompting. The disciples will want training for effective outreach simply because they have initiated a redemptive relationship with a seeking unbeliever. The question first orients the Christian to the Great Commission as an integral issue of godly character. The initial accountability gets the ball rolling. They are then involved in the process with real people through relationship, which often leads to questions and discussions. As a result, they are open to further training. This is a far more effective flow for learning evangelism than most training methods offered today. It involves them in evangelism first, then once they have begun a "redemptive relationship," they will discover a need for help and will be better students for any evangelism training they receive.

Since we have published the first resource that includes Life Transformation Groups, *Raising Leaders for the Harvest*, I have made a point of collecting sample questions I have encountered across the country. I have included them with some other historic lists of questions in the first appendix of this book. My hope is that this will stimulate your own thinking and you can come up with the best questions for your own context.

3. How do they answer the questions that arise from the reading?

One of the important steps for our church was to grant people permission to say, "I don't know," without feeling ashamed. Only when we are willing to admit that we don't know something are we going to be able to learn something.

One thing that will astound you is the way that the growing disciples are able to find answers to their own questions when they read the same passage of Scripture repetitively.

I had one man I met with each week who wanted to take advantage of meeting with the pastor. It was his chance to try and "stump the pastor." In his first reading of Ephesians each week he would take out a small tablet and write down any questions he would have. After that he would just read the book however many times we were supposed to. When we would meet on Wednesday mornings he would flip the tablet open like a detective on *Dragnet* and fire away on an unsuspecting pastor with his questions. What would occur each week was remarkable! He would go to the first question with great enthusiasm, sure that he would confound my great wisdom, but before he could finish reading the question his countenance would drop some and he would remark, "Oh, I think I know the answer to that question." Then he would go to the next question and the same thing would happen. This went on for several weeks until finally, he realized he could understand the Bible himself and he began his own LTG. This LTG multiplied faster than any other I have ever been involved with. In less than four months it had multiplied, and by conversion growth at that!

What happened is that he would write out the questions the first time he would read through the book that week. Since we were reading it five times in a week, by the end of the week he would understand the book enough to answer his own questions. I enjoyed watching him realize that he could read the Bible himself and that he didn't need a pastor to interpret it for him.

Of course, not every question will be answered in this manner. Aside from learning to be comfortable not having all the answers, there are some helpful books available which people can use. I have suggested to others that they use the following:

- Inter Varsity Press has a series of books called the *Hard sayings of ... the Old Testament*; *Jesus*; *Paul*.[32]

- Gleason Archer has written a book called, *Encyclopedia of Bible Difficulties*. This is one volume and very helpful.[33]

Written by evangelical scholars, these books will address many of the questions that are raised without having to add a middleman because they are reference books rather than curricula. The questions that are raised come from the Christian's own study of and reflection on the Scriptures. We do recommend, however, that the groups be encouraged to discover the answers, using just the Scriptures themselves, before these reference books are used. Challenge people to think and grapple with the Scriptures before you point them to a quick and articulate answer from someone else. You may find, as we have, that these resources are not in as high a demand as expected.

4. What do they talk about at a typical LTG meeting?

The accountability questions can stimulate great interaction. Men and women will find it liberating to talk freely about things that they previously felt ashamed to discuss. Where they once thought they were alone with unique struggles, they suddenly discover that they have common ground, and the group can exchange helpful ideas to overcome their temptations. There is power in a group of two or three working together as a team to overcome sin!

Often the passage being read by the group stimulates discussion. The accountability questions themselves (question 9) lead naturally into a discussion of the application of the truth to their own lives from the reading they've done. Group members can bring up questions that were raised, applications that came to mind during the week, or inspiring words that meant something special.

I have intentionally kept the groups from having any other agenda than reading the word, confessing sins with the questions and praying. I have found that the people in the groups have no problem coming up with something meaningful to talk about. In fact, many of the groups I've been a part of have found it hard to end the meeting and get to work on time. I've actually had one man come up with his own accountability question that read, "Have you made it to work on time every day this week?" We did our best after that to make sure that he was on time the morning that he met with us.

5. How do I get these groups started in my church?

We recommend that you initiate these groups more organically than organizationally. In other words, don't just start with your elder/deacon board and hope the strategy will trickle its way down to the masses. The place to start is at the grass roots—you and a new believer, a seeker, or a Christian who desperately needs help. Then you can increase the number of groups in two ways: (1) by multiplying your own groups, and (2) adding new groups by giving people copies of this book and telling others how they work. Whenever a person who needs spiritual growth comes along, introduce them to another Christian and explain how you recommend that they help one another using this simple system. Follow up with them in three to four weeks and inquire as to how they are implementing the system. In these kinds of groups, follow up is especially important because the group members have not had any experience of their own in the LTG process in order to orient themselves, so more directive instruction is usually needed.

It is not hard to find people who need Christ and are desiring His help. The LTG's provide a natural connection for those who seek counseling, those who need to transition from a twelve-step group, or even those who return from a Promise Keepers rally full of energy and zeal. It is also a natural follow up for new believers. LTG's can provide the needed balance and substance to follow up with those who come to Christ at large crusades.

Once the groups start to grow and multiply, they can incite a godly jealousy in a congregation, who see the new life in other members and hunger for a transformation of their own.

The LTG's can also be a great means for winning new souls to Christ! Friends, neighbors, co-workers or family members who want help can come to meet the Savior in a context of hearing directly from God through the Scriptures and coming to terms with their own sin in a confidential relationship of accountability. It is very refreshing for seekers to find Christians who aren't perfect and know it! The LTG's are a quest for righteousness in a context of mutual love and support. There is hardly a better place to introduce new babes to the kingdom!

6. How long will these groups last?

The LTG's are living things that have their own life span. Some have lasted as long as three years, others have multiplied in as short a time as one month! Believe it or not, it is more frequent to see multiplication occur sooner than later! If a group does not multiply in the first year, the chances are that it will not. Don't let that concern you too greatly; you have all benefited by implementing important spiritual disciplines. You have also received a system that you can continue to use in your life. If you do find, however, that you have a group that is not multiplying after a year of faithful participation, we recommend that you look to start another quickly and initiate multiplication yourself.

Because these groups implant the true seed, rather than a seed substitute, multiplication rarely needs to be forced, coerced, or manipulated. In fact, our experience has shown that it doesn't usually need to be mentioned at all! It is good to cast vision for multiplication, but the real impetus for it comes from the seed itself, germinated in good soil.

A group will end in one of two ways: it will give birth to one or two other groups, or it will die. Both will happen, both are to be expected. Read the parable of the sower again (Mark 4:1-20)! You will see that there are four kinds of soil, which have four different responses to the gospel, only one of which was fruitful. If you are in a group, and it dies, don't be to discouraged. Try again. The fruit you will see in the end will far outweigh any discouragement.

Chapter 12:
Troubleshooting
Unproductive Groups

Since Life Transformation Groups have been at work around the world I have had a chance to dialogue with many new practitioners. Often when I am told that the groups are less effective I find that there are a few ways in which the principles shared in this book have been compromised in some way. Typically there are four errors which slow the process down. You will find that what I share in this chapter repeats some of what I have already shared but if you are having less than productive results, chances are that these principles bear repeating.

1. Reduced Scripture Intake Syndrome

When someone tells me that the groups just aren't working, the first question I usually ask is, "How much Bible reading are you doing each week?" Often the reading has been cut down, usually to about five to fifteen chapters each week. The word of God is what changes people's hearts (Heb. 4:12). When we cut back on its intake we slow down the transformation process. It's that simple. More Word, more transformation. Less Word, less transformation. If you want to see the kind of spontaneous multiplication I have described in this book you can't compromise on the intake of God's Word.

2. Poor Disciple Selection Syndrome

The second area I often find that has been compromised is in the selection of disciples. It is very important to find desperate sinners if we want to make disciples. The more desperate they are the more their lives will change. If you start with saintly Christians you shouldn't be surprised if you don't see much change in their lives because there isn't much there to change. Jesus didn't start with the good religious people. He started with the common sinners who had a rough edge to them. Later, after His disciples started blossoming into leaders, religious leaders started coming. First, Nicodemus; later, Joseph of Arimathea; last of all, as if untimely born, Saul of Tarsus. Eventually many religious people came into the movement (Acts 6:7), but there was both a blessing and a problem with these men (Acts 15:5). Try to imagine how profoundly different Christianity would've been if Jesus started with religious leaders. It would have been like putting new wine into old wineskins and it would've burst and spilled its precious contents.

I have intentionally left the criteria for selecting candidates for the kingdom very simple so that it is easy to remember (it is also very Biblical). The question is often asked, "Should I start with Christians or non-Christians?" That is not the right question to ask. The place to start is with a desperate need that only Jesus can meet—whether that person is a Christian or not. Often, pastors will give in to the temptation to start with their leaders, and then will find the results less than dramatic, give up on the system and go back to whatever they were doing before.

It is common sense that shows us that if we start with "already committed Christian leaders" we will see less life change than if we start with desperate sinners—there is less to change. I understand the desire to implement accountability among leaders and the temptation to influence the entire church by starting with her leaders. You will probably be able to do just that in time if you start with desperate sinners first and let the leaders see it work in others first. Let a godly jealousy emerge in the heart of your leaders as they watch lost causes become men and women consumed with a cause. They will notice and some may desire the same transformation. If not, you may end up with new leaders in a few leaders who are capable, faithful and on fire with a love for Jesus and others.

If you simply must implement this with your leaders initially, I suggest that you also start a second group with a couple of desperate sinners as well. This may give you a chance to test the substance of your leaders and also test the truth of what I am expounding in this book. The comparison of the two groups may teach you a lot. If I am right you've only gained and if you are right you have gained again.

3. Leadership Intrusion Syndrome

A third area where the system is often compromised is in the addition of supplemental material or a more defined leadership role. As bad as it sounds, pastors often don't trust the Holy Spirit and the Word of God to do what they do best. Instead they tend to get in the way with "better stuff" and find that the whole process is lacking. They would never admit this, even to themselves, but they do betray this misplaced belief in actions. This is a natural temptation but it should be resisted. Faith in God and His word will never end in disappointment (Romans 10:11)! Leadership will emerge in groups naturally, but when it invades a group unnaturally it tends to hijack all the natural process that these groups can create.

4. Programatic Implementation Syndrome

A fourth reason why LTG's may not succeed in some churches is because they are implemented as a program instead of a grass roots system. Pastors, eager to find a solution to ministry demands, sometimes will apply this system as a blanket program for everyone, often assigning accountability partners. This approach goes directly against many of the values and principles shared in this book. You may find that this works in some cases, but it is not the recommended method of implementation. The system works much better if natural relationships are formed and the influence of LTG's is allowed to develop organically.

If you must implement it as a program, my suggestion is that you also initiate a group or groups in a more organic fashion as well. I think you will probably find these other groups, begun more naturally, become a base of real change in your church. The danger with approaching the LTG's as a blanket program for the whole church is that if the first attempt doesn't see immediate results (which is likely given the amount of compromise to these principles) then the system is thrown out. The church is then left feeling like, "We've tried that before and it didn't work," when in fact they did not truly give it a fair trial.

If you find that you are not experiencing the kind of transformation mentioned in this book, go back over these principles and see if there is a place where you have compromised one or more of them. Before you write off this book and all that is in it, examine what you're doing and see if it indeed matches what I have expounded. You may choose to adapt and change some of the methodology because you don't buy in to all my values, or have some others that you need to take into account. That is fine; just realize that these principles work and the more you diminish them, the more you diminish the results.

If the methodology that I have explained doesn't fit you or your context, that is fine. I suggest that you take the principles that I have expounded and see if you can develop a method that embraces them and works for you. The method is not what changes lives, it is the Spirit of God and His Biblical principles that transform people.

I recently sat across the table from a young leader who told me that the groups hadn't seen the results he'd expected after listening to one of my audiotapes on the subject. I asked him the usual questions and found that he hadn't compromised any of the principles and seemed to understand and value them. Finally, I asked him how long they had been meeting. He said with a degree of exasperation, "Over a month now!" I must say, I was challenged by his faith. I told him to be patient and keep plugging on.

Don't expect to change the world in a month—a generation, maybe, but not a month. The saying is true, "We tend to overestimate what we can do in a year and underestimate what we can do in five." Remember that multiplication begins slowly and gains momentum as it goes.

Keep in mind, as well, that not every group will have the same results. Some will never multiply while others may multiply countless times in a short period of time. Jesus told us that there were four kinds of soil and only one was good soil and produced fruit (Mark 4:3-20). Expect to lose some of your seed in less than fertile soil. Remember, as well, that there were three different capacities of good soil: those that produced thirty-fold fruit, those that produced sixty-fold, and those that produced one hundred-fold fruit (Mark 4:8). All fruitfulness is good; not all is the same.

Chapter 13:
Conclusion—
Church according to Jesus

As director of the church planting efforts of my denomination in the Southwest district of the United States, I once had to meet with one of our churches for an emergency consultation. The church was struggling with leadership issues and I ended up interviewing a good number of those in the church. The main issue was a desire to have a constitution and by-laws that would enable the church to be recognized by our particular denomination. Apparently, many felt that they weren't a church until this took place. The church planter felt that other areas of growth and development were more important at that time and was at odds with some of the people in the church over this.

At one point I needed a nice quiet time alone with the Lord so I went out to lunch by myself. I sat down asking the Lord one of the most important questions I have ever asked, "What makes a church a church?"

As I sat at the restaurant a friendly waitress came up to take my order. As she was about to leave, I noticed that she was wearing a ring on her hand that had a fish symbol on it. I thought, "Isn't that just like the Lord to encourage me and address my concerns by sending a sister in the Lord to my table and showing me that the true church is much more than these petty concerns."

The fish symbol has been a symbol of Christ from the early days of the church. It began when the church was under horrendous persecution and was driven underground, literally, into the catacombs. During those days of intense persecution, the Christians began a tradition of drawing an arc in the dirt with a walking stick or their toe. If the other person drew a second arc opposite of the first completing a fish shape, then they both knew that they were Christians and that they could fellowship freely without concern of persecution. The fish sign is still a mark used to identify believers even to this day.

I decided to ask this waitress about her faith when she returned.

She came back to the table with my food and I said to her, "I noticed that you have a fish symbol on your ring—are you a Christian?"

She said, "No, I'm a Pisces."

Ouch! While it wasn't what I expected, the Lord did help to answer my concerns. The church is not to be identified by bumper stickers or fish signs any more than constitutions and by-laws. It isn't a steeple on the top of a building or a sign in the front that says "church" on it that is to identify the true church of Jesus Christ. Jesus said it was our "love one for another" that would identify us as His.

This experience sent me into a discovery process to find out what church is according to Jesus. He really only mentions the word "church" twice, but I think that we can learn a lot about what church is supposed to be like by examining what He had to say in Matthew chapter 16, verses 13 to18.

The first time Jesus mentions the church is while He and His disciples went to Caesarea Philippi on a retreat together. Jesus gave the disciples a "pop quiz". There is a good reason why teachers like to give pop quizzes. A pop quiz truly reveals what you know.

The first question of the quiz was easy, "Who do people say that I am?" This one was fun for the disciples to answer. Everyone jumped in to the discussion each with their own theories. It is always easy to carry on about the mistakes of others. But, what the disciples didn't realize was that this was only a warm up question.

The second question was the real test. This is the most important question anyone will ever answer, and our eternal destiny hangs in the balance. Jesus then asked, "But who do *you* say that I am (emphasis mine)? " The Scriptures don't tell us this, but I can imagine that it suddenly got real quiet. I can also picture all the eyes that were so on fire with enthusiasm a moment earlier were now falling slowly to the ground. This question is much harder to answer because it is personal—if you get it wrong, it is you who are at fault.

The weight of the importance of this question made the air thick with tension. I can imagine all the disciples slowly turning their heads in Peter's direction just hoping that he would speak up as he often did and thus get them all off the hook. Peter, probably very uncomfortable with silence, was ready to oblige. In one special moment he lifted his voice with boldness and a sense of power and said, "Thou art the Christ, the son of the living God."

Jesus must have smiled at that moment, and the tension instantly lifted. Peter must have felt a surge of pride (he would later need to be humbled). Jesus was then to give Peter a blessing that would touch his life forever. Jesus said, "Blessed are you Simon Barjona, because flesh and blood did not reveal that to you but My Father who is in heaven."

Peter got it right, but he needed help to do so. All of us need help from heaven if we are to know Jesus. We don't get there by having a higher IQ or studying the right books. It isn't intelligence that gets us to heaven, it is the grace of God. Only if we accept His help can we truly know Jesus.

The verse I really want to focus on is verse 18, but I begin with the context above because that is where Jesus began. It is the right place to begin when we talk of what the church truly is. Everything about church begins and ends with who Jesus is. Jesus' statement about the church has a context that begins with God's grace revealing the identity of Jesus and ends with the work of Christ on the cross and His awesome resurrection three days later (Matt. 16:21). If we get everything else right and skip this important question then we are not truly the church. Church begins with Jesus—who He is and what He has done. It is all about Jesus and if it begins to be about something else, then it stops being the church as Jesus meant it to be.

Jesus went on to say, "And I also say to you that you are Peter, and upon this rock I will build My church; and the gates of Hades shall not overpower it." There are five things I want you to see about the church according to Jesus:

1. Jesus builds the church.

There are many books, tapes, seminars and CD's that are made to help people build the church, but if you're building the church it isn't the church. He didn't say, "... and upon this rock you will build my church." Jesus, and only Jesus, builds the church. If we build a church based on a charismatic personality, an innovative methodology or anything else we have a church that is inferior to that which Jesus would build.

2. Jesus owns the church.

He bought her with His own blood. He didn't promise that He "...will build *your* church." The church belongs to Jesus. He is building His church.

I once read a story about a contractor who built homes in a small town. He built most of the homes for people who lived in the town and was a very gifted carpenter. Unfortunately he was never able to afford a home of his own. One day, the wealthiest man in town came to the contractor and asked him to build a house for him. He said, "I want you to build the finest house you are capable of, and I want you to spare no expense. I am going on a journey and when I return I hope that the house is completed."

The contractor agreed to the job and was about to begin when a thought struck him, "I will use inferior material, do a quick and sloppy job on the house, make it look real nice and charge him the full amount. That way I can pocket the leftover money and finally afford to buy my own house." This is what he did.

When the rich man returned he went to view the house and was very impressed. It looked beautiful from a distance. The wealthy man turned to the crooked contractor and said, "The house looks wonderful! I am so glad that you spared no expense for I intend to give this home to a dear friend." With that, he handed the keys over to the contractor and said "Here is your new home, my friend." The contractor graciously received the keys to his new home but his heart sank as he realized what he had done.

What kind of effort and quality of workmanship and materials would the man have put into the home if he knew that it would be the place where he and his family would be living? The church is Jesus' building project and He fully intends to live in it. When Jesus is at work building His church it will be beautiful and solid. He doesn't do sloppy work. If our churches are falling apart and are not healthy it is not because Jesus has done a poor job, but because we have taken the task upon ourselves.

3. The church is meant to be growing.

Everyone has driven by a building that is being built. None of us have driven a second time by the construction and found it to be smaller the next time. When something is being built it grows bigger, not smaller. Jesus is building His church and it should be growing. The church is meant to grow. She should experience spiritual growth, and seeing new souls brought into the kingdom of God is part of that.

4. The church that is growing will face opposition.

Jesus said that we would face resistance when the church starts to grow. He identified the antagonism as that which comes from Hades. Wherever the church is alive and growing, hell is opposing it.

One sign of a healthy church is that she faces hostility from hell. One preacher has said, "If you wake up in the morning and don't run into the enemy head on, then maybe you're going in the wrong direction." Ed Silvoso rightly points out that the Bible doesn't say to ignore the devil and he will flee from you.[34] We must stand firm and resist the enemy.

In *Releasing Your Church's Potential*, Tom Clegg has said, "I believe that the enemy divides all people into two categories, those he can ignore and those he has to fight. I want to be one of those that he has to fight." He went on to quote a friend of his who was a WWII bomber pilot: "If you're receiving flack you're over the target."[35]

5. The church that Jesus builds is unstoppable!

The enemy we face is powerful. He has been around from the beginning of time and has been a constant study of human nature. His first attempt to destroy human life was against a man and a woman who were stronger and purer than we are—he succeeded. He has been perfecting his craft ever since. He knows each of our weaknesses and vulnerabilities. He has an army of soldiers at his command. He and all of his forces are invisible and surround us.

When I try to picture our situation in this light I begin to see church as a refuge or shelter. I see her as a fortress where we are defending the saints from the vicious wolf pack who surrounds us and wants to devour each of us. But this description of church does not fit the one given by Jesus in this verse.

Jesus said that the gates of hell shall *not* prevail against His church. It dawned on me one day that a gate is not an offensive weapon. Police don't pack loaded gates. Postal workers don't go crazy with semi-automatic gates. Terrorists don't hold victims at gate-point. Dogs don't run loose with little signs around their necks that read "Beware of Gate."

Gates are not a threat, they are defensive, and the gates Jesus was talking about aren't pearly ones—they're the gates of *hell*! The church is to be on the offense, not defense. The church has been held hostage at gate-point for far too long. It is time that we stop being intimidated by a gate!

The Western church, unfortunately, is usually in a defensive posture. We are threatened by the whole alphabet, from ABC to CBS to NBC. We don't trust the IRS, the CIA or the FBI. We are threatened by the ACLU, and the NAACP. We defend ourselves against the LDS' and the JW's as if our backs are against the wall. If this is not enough, we are often threatened by one another! Some of us don't feel comfortable unless we are in defense as if being on offense is a sin. We are so defensive that it's offensive!

Can you imagine what would happen if the Denver Broncos decided to bring only their defensive unit to play against the Green Bay Packers in the Super Bowl? No matter how good their defense plays, they could never win without scoring some points.

I was once playing chess with a ten-year-old boy. This was his first time playing the game. We were evenly matched. Near the end of the game he had lost his queen and I began to chase his king all over the board. He would make a move then I would move—"check". He would move, I would move—"check". He'd move, I'd move—"check". This went on for a while and I began to wonder how this game would ever end. While I was daydreaming in my self-confidence, the boy was strategizing. The trap was set. The trap was sprung. My queen was gone and he was in charge of the board. I instantly went from offense to defense. I would move, he would move—"check". I'd move, he'd move—"check." Big hearted as I am, I eventually let the boy win.

Like that boy, the church today needs to make a similar switch from defense to offense if we are to be all that Jesus intends.

A few years ago I was going to France to conduct some leadership seminars for missionaries in Europe. Before traveling, I visited a party with some friends and family members to celebrate the birth of a new child. Dana and I were the only Christians at the party. A friend of ours there heard that we would be in Paris and she began to urge us to go to the Rodin museum.

Rodin was a French impressionist sculptor. Though many do not recognize his name, most are familiar with his work. He created the Thinker. What you may not realize is that the Thinker was really a study he had done to sit on the top of his greatest masterpiece—the Gates of Hell. For years we have been wondering what it is that the Thinker is thinking about. No, he's not wondering where he left his clothes the night before. What the Thinker is contemplating is an eternity of judgement separated from God.

My friend at the party began to describe the Gates of Hell for us. It is a tall, haunting work with countless figures writhing in pain and agony sliding down into their judgement with the Thinker sitting above it all with a mood of regret and contemplation. As she started to picture it she got caught up in appreciation for it and said in amazement, "Oh, I could just stare at the Gates of Hell forever."

There was a long pause in the conversation as her words began to sink in. A few gave an uncomfortable chuckle as it dawned on them how significant her words truly were. All I could think of to say at that moment was "Oh, I hope not."

This adequately sums up for us the cost of the church remaining in a passive, defensive posture. When we sit back in our fortress frightened by all that seems to threaten us we let countless souls remain captive to the forces of hell. We need to turn from defense to offense and storm the gates to set the captives free. This is church according to Jesus.

The church is a vibrant, authentic expression of Jesus' love and truth in this dark world, and with Jesus at the helm, she is unstoppable!

Summary

How can I release spontaneous multiplication of growing disciples in my church? Fruitfulness begins with the right seed in the right soil. The Life Transformation Group System can be the catalyst to release real spontaneous multiplication of disciples in your own ministry environment but it requires that you begin the process. If your own life can't be transformed first, you have no right to expect to transform another's.

There is a cost involved with multiplication. For the salmon the cost is death. It swims upstream, lays its eggs in the sand and then dies.

Grain also dies to reproduce. Jesus said,

> Truly, truly, I say to you, unless a grain of wheat falls into the earth and dies, it remains by itself alone; but if it dies, it bears much fruit. He who loves his life loses it; and he who hates his life in this world shall keep it to life eternal (John 12:24).

As disciples, we must deny ourselves and pick up our cross and follow Christ. This is all about surrender. This is about confession and repentance. This is about obedience. Where these things exist there is a dying of self and reproduction will come.

We've got to be willing to give up more than our time, talents and treasure— we've got to start by giving up our lives for the sake of His kingdom. If we are willing to pay the price—if we are willing to die to follow Christ—then we can see an abundant harvest of souls for the kingdom of God. The church of the first century was willing to give their lives for the expansion of the kingdom and they were able to reach the entire known world with the gospel. Every church throughout history that was willing to surrender their lives for the sake of Christ witnessed dramatic and spontaneous growth. This is one reason why churches thrive under persecution—the people of God are forced to decide what really matters most. They count the cost and pay the price. They die to themselves, and their spiritual lives reproduce, and church growth occurs through multiplication.

I have heard that scientific and statistical probabilities have demonstrated that if a single shaft of wheat is left unmarred and blighted and allowed to freely reproduce and grow, within only eight years it will have multiplied into a crop large enough to feed the entire world population—for an entire year!

How long will it take to reach the world through multiplication? If every Christian were to lead just one person to Christ every year, and disciple that person so that he would in turn do the same the next year, it would only take about thirty five years to reach the entire world for Christ! Has the thought ever occurred to you that we are only one generation away from extinction? If we all failed to reproduce ourselves, and pass the torch of life into the hands of the next generation, Christianity would be over in just one generation. Yet, because of the POWER of multiplication, we are also just one generation away from worldwide fulfillment of the Great Commission— the choice is ours.

Appendix 1:
Sample Character
Conversation Questions for
Life Transformation Groups

The use of questions for accountability is not a new idea. I have been collecting samples of such questions for a few years and have included these to give you some more ideas of how you can keep yourself accountable for a godly life.

There are advantages and disadvantages with any system. Of note there are a few very common concerns that I will briefly address when applying accountability questions of any type.

Legalism

Legalism is a very severe threat for the church and is not treated lightly in the Scriptures. There is no other sin in the New Testament that receives a more severe condemnation. Think about that a moment—no other sin! It is not unusual for people to use a man-made system of accountability as a measure for righteousness. This has tragic results that should always be avoided. The intent of questions is not to define what sin and righteousness are but to be a platform for opening up discussion about what is going on in one's character development. Some of the questions below do a better job than others at being cautious to not provide a man made standard of behavior.

Open-ended vs . Closed-ended Questions

Some have found that the published questions that this book suggests are closed ended and less conducive to stimulate conversation, so they have developed more open-ended questions. Experience has shown that only one question on the list has solicited a curt "yes" or "no" answer: "Have you given in to an addictive behavior this past week?" For that reason we added the simple statement: "Explain", which seems to have helped. It is probably true that having more open-ended questions will promote more elaboration and discussion. The balance here is that most LTG meetings are pressed to keep to an hour as it is. Again, your preference should prevail considering these balanced perspectives.

Evangelism Incorporated in Spiritual Formation

We have found that including a question that brings up the subject of being a testimony of Christ in word and in deed does much for the growth and reproduction of any group. When the spread of the Good News of Christ is included in character formation, spiritual growth is accelerated and reproduction is often the result. This has been proven over and over again in the course of using accountability questions. It can be argued that simply turning the focus of the group inside out—to the needs and concerns of the lost—rather than remaining internally directed is what separates LTG's from being just another accountability group. There is definitely a difference between an accountability group, which strives to manage sinful behavior, and a Life Transformation Group that capitalizes on new life and produces growth and reproduction of disciples. The idea that one can grow in character and not fulfill the great commission is a curious concept to say the least. I do believe that we as a people have fallen under a delusion that character is separate from obedience to the basic command of Scripture in this regard. For those who live under the constant threat of real persecution being a testimony for Christ is a significant part of their Christian character. For them, though their life is on the line, they will not compromise their character or their obedience. This shames those of us in the western church that do not live under such a threat and yet are fearful of speaking up in the market place or neighborhood.

Listening to God's Voice

Personal connection to the Lord is a very real concern behind many of the sample questions below, and rightfully so. When questions are less specific in behavior, they need to include some question that keeps the participant listening to the guiding presence of the Holy Spirit. It is rightfully believed that such will infect behavior with the same result but with the added benefit of hearing it from God rather than a list of questions on a card. I commend those who have thought this through and revised the questions in this way.

There is perhaps a balance to be found in this regard. It is suggested that newer believers and pre-Christians use the more specific questions and that after some growth and maturity is evident the less specific questions may enhance the confession of sin. The difficulty with this is that I do find it very healthy and important for those with maturity to be in groups that have seekers and newer believers in them. The key is to understand that the questions are to be a helpful tool as we get started in listening to the Lord and sharing the struggles each is going through in their own walk with the Savior.

As you read through the variety of Character Conversation Questions listed below, keep these observations in mind. Look for the strengths and weaknesses of each set of questions and you will be better prepared to choose or create questions that best fit your own needs.

Sample Accountability Questions:

John Wesley's Small Group Questions:

A popularized version of Wesley's Holy Club Questions:

1. Am I consciously or unconsciously creating the impression that I am better than I am? In other words, am I a hypocrite?

2. Am I honest in all my acts and words, or do I exaggerate?

3. Do I confidentially pass onto another what was told me in confidence?

4. Am I a slave to dress, friends, work, or habits?

5. Am I self-conscious, self-pitying, or self-justifying?

6. Did the Bible live in me today?

7. Do I give it time to speak to me everyday?

8. Am I enjoying prayer?

9. When did I last speak to someone about my faith?

10. Do I pray about the money I spend?

11. Do I get to bed on time and get up on time?

12. Do I disobey God in anything?

13. Do I insist upon doing something about which my conscience is uneasy?

14. Am I defeated in any part of my life?

15. Am I jealous, impure, critical, irritable, touchy or distrustful?

16. How do I spend my spare time?

17. Am I proud?

18. Do I thank God that I am not as other people, especially as the Pharisee who despised the publican?

19. Is there anyone whom I fear, dislike, disown, criticize, hold resentment toward or disregard? If so, what am I going to do about it?

20. Do I grumble and complain constantly?

21. Is Christ real to me?

Wesley's Band Meeting Questions:

1. What known sins have you committed since our last meeting?

2. What temptations have you met with?

3. How were you delivered?

4. What have you thought, said, or done, of which you doubt whether it be sin or not?

5. Have you nothing you desire to keep secret?

Reference: John Wesley's Class Meetings: a Model for Making Disciples, by D. Michael Henderson, Evangel Publishing House, 1997, pp.118-9

Chuck Swindoll's Pastoral Accountability Questions:

In his book, *The Body*, by Chuck Colson (p. 131), a list of seven questions used by Chuck Swindoll and a small group of pastors is listed.

1. Have you been with a woman anywhere this past week that might be seen as compromising?

2. Have any of your financial dealings lacked integrity?

3. Have you exposed yourself to any sexually explicit material?

4. Have you spent adequate time in Bible study and prayer?

5. Have you given priority time to your family?

6. Have you fulfilled the mandates of your calling?

7. Have you just lied to me?

Renovare Questions:

James Bryan Smith and Richard Foster have compiled a list of questions for accountability to spiritual disciplines which is a part of the Renovare resources.

1. In what ways did God make his presence known to you since our last meeting? What experiences of prayer, meditation and spiritual reading has God given you? What difficulties or frustrations did you encounter? What joys or delights?

2. What temptations did you face since our last meeting? How did you respond? Which spiritual disciplines did God use to lead you further into holiness of heart and life?

3. Have you sensed any influence or work of the Holy Spirit since our last meeting? What spiritual gifts did the Spirit enable you to exercise? What was the outcome? What fruit of the Spirit would you like to see increase in your life? Which disciplines might be useful in this effort?

4. What opportunities did God give you to serve others since our last meeting? How did you respond? Did you encounter injustice to or oppression of others? Were you able to work for justice and shalom?

5. In what ways did you encounter Christ in your reading of the Scripture since our last meeting? How has the Bible shaped the way you think and live? Did God provide an opportunity for you to share your faith with someone? How did you respond?

Sample LTG questions adapted since the original publication:

Phil Helfer, pastor of Los Altos Brethren Church in Long Beach, CA, has simplified the LTG questions into "Five Basic Questions":

1. How have you experienced God in your life this week?

2. What is God teaching you?

3. How are you responding to His prompting?

4. Do you have a need to confess any sin?

5. How did you do with your reading this week?

A church in Palo Alto, CA, called The Highway Community, has adapted the questions in the following way:

1. Did I invest the proper quality/quantity of time in my most important relationships?

2. Did my life reflect verbal integrity?

3. Did I express a forgiving attitude toward others?

4. Did I practice undisciplined or addictive behavior?

5. Was I honorable in my financial dealings?

6. Was I sexually pure?

7. Did I spend time with the Lord this week, completing the Bible reading for the week?

8. Did I pray for my pre-Christian friends? Did I talk with someone about Christ?

In an attempt to bring the authority of Scripture into personal obedience and growth, Florent Varak, a French pastor in Lyon, has developed these questions:

1. What have the Scriptures revealed in your life this week:

    - In terms of specific sinful behavior?

    - In terms of specific sinful thoughts?

    - In terms of specific sinful words?

2. What errors or lies that you once believed have now been corrected by your reading of the Scriptures?

3. What encouragement have the Scriptures given you in your daily walk?

4. What do you need to ask the Spirit of God to reveal to you that you have not yet understood?

Recently some children have asked if they could be a part of the Life Transformation Groups. I challenged Lori Dillman, a mom in our church to help me come up with a set of questions appropriate for pre-adolescent kids. These are the questions we have come up with:

1. How have your actions and words shown others that you love Jesus?

2. How have you been respectful to your parents and the adults around you this week?

3. How have you loved others even when you didn't feel like it?

4. How have you seen God answer your prayers this past week?

5. In what ways have you been angry or frustrated this week because you didn't get something that you wanted or didn't get your way?

6. In what ways have you taken anything that does not belong to you this week?

7. In what ways have you not told the truth this week?

8. In what ways have you been mean to others this week?

9. In what ways have you not completed the responsibilities you have been given?

10. Have you finished your Bible reading? What did you learn?

Working on a list of questions that are less specific I came up with this list:

1. What is the condition of your soul?

2. What sin do you need to confess?

3. What have you held back from God that you need to surrender?

4. Is there anything that has dampened your zeal for Christ?

5. Who have you talked with about Christ this week?

As a church planting missionary in Buenos Aires, Argentina, Dave Guiles (currently the director of Grace Brethren International Missions) developed these questions based loosely on the tests of a true believer found in 1 John:

1. How have you sensed God's presence in your life during this past week?

2. Have you received specific answer to your prayers? What was it?

3. Have you spoken with a non-believer about your faith in Jesus Christ? With whom?

4. To whom have you shown God's love during this past week?

5. What have you learned about God in your personal Bible reading this past week?

6. As a result of your Bible reading this past week, how have you determined to better obey God?

7. Specifically, what area of your life do you feel that God most wants to change? Have you taken specific steps to make those changes?

8. What good habit do you feel God wants to form in your life? Have you taken specific steps to develop that habit?

Paul Klawitter a church planting missionary in France has developed the following questions:

1. What worries or other issues are you currently facing?

2. Is there an area that God is working on in your life or any sin that you would like to pray about?

3. For what non-Christian friends can we pray?

4. In your reading of the Bible: Who is God? What does He expect of you? What do you think He is saying to you? How do you think you should respond.

The most simplified and basic questions I have found to date is a list of two:

1. What is God telling you to do?

2. What are you going to do about it?

Appendix 2:
Other Names Given to Life
Transformation Groups
around the World

We have encouraged others to make the Life Transformation Group their own. In so doing I have often challenged people to name it something that works well in their own context. Below is a list of the variety of names I have come across in recent years:

My own original name for the method was Bible Impact Groups (BIGs). There are still many churches where this name has stuck.

Bible Impact Groups (BIG's)—Grace Fellowship of Alta Loma, CA (and many other churches)

Commitment to Grow Groups (CTG groups)—All over Latin America and now the U.S.

Growth Groups—New Song Church, Covina, CA (and several other churches)

Spiritual Triads—Dijon, France

Link Groups—Highway Community Church, Palo Alto, CA

Anchor Groups—The Harbor Church, Orlando, FL

For More Information
Contact...

Life Transformation Groups are a foundational part of our larger strategy for a church multiplication movement, which seeks to apply the same values of being biblically consistent, outreach-oriented, reproducible, transferable and relationally accountable. For a more comprehensive understanding of a church based leadership developmental system that reflects these same values and results in raising leaders from the harvest for the harvest check out *Raising Leaders for the Harvest* co-authored by Robert E. Logan and Neil Cole. This resource and more are available through either of the following organizations:

ChurchSmart Resources is an evangelical Christian publisher committed to producing excellent products at affordable prices to help church leaders accomplish effective ministry in the areas of Church planting, Church growth, Church renewal and leadership development. For a free catalog of our resources call 1-800-253-4276 or visit our web site at www.ChurchSmart.com.

Church Multiplication Associates and CMA Resources is a kingdom extension ministry of the Grace Brethren Churches of Southern California and Arizona. Our mission is to facilitate a church multiplication movement by focusing resources on reproducing disciples, leaders, ministries and churches. We develop resources; train, assess, deploy and coach church planters in the harvest; and help cast vision to rethink how the church can get back to her mission. For a free catalog of our resources or to discover more about our ministry, call us toll-free at (877) 732-3593 or log on to our web page at www.CMAResources.com.

End Notes

Introduction

[1] Swindoll, Charles R.; *Dropping Your Guard*, Word, p. 121

[2] Ibid

[3] Logan, Robert; Cole, Neil; *Raising Leaders for the Harvest*, ChurchSmart Resources, pp. 1-4

[4] Barna, George; *Evangelism That Works*, Regal, p. 22

[5] Barna, George; *Evangelism That Works,* Regal, p. 38

[6] Arn, Charles; "A Response to Dr. Rainer: What is the Key to Effective Evangelism", *Journal of the American Society for Church Growth*, Vol. 6, 1995, p. 74

[7] Ibid

[8] Clegg, Tom; from seminar given titled, "How to Plant a Church"

[9] Silvoso, Ed; *That None Should Perish*, Regal, 1994, p. 72

[10] This is found in the *Mishnah*, see Shabbath 7:2

[11] Colson, Charles; *Loving God*, Zondervan, pp. 24-25

[12] Colson, Charles; *Loving God*, Zondervan, p. 25

[13] Henrichsen, Walter A.; *Disciples are Made—not Born: Making Disciples Out of Christians*, Victor, p. 143

[14] Schwarz, Christian A.; Schalk, Christoph; *Implementation Guide to Natural Church Development*, ChurchSmart Resources, p. 136

[15] Henrichsen, Walter A.; *Disciples are Made—not Born: Making Disciples Out of Christians*, Victor, p. 142

[16] Ibid, p. 142

[17] Schwarz, Christian A.; Schalk, Christoph; *Implementation Guide to Natural Church Development*, ChurchSmart Resources, p. 136

[18] Ibid

[19] Bounds, E.M.; *Power Through Prayer*, p. 8

[20] Warren, Rick; *The Purpose Driven Church*, Zondervan, p. 32

[21] Los Angeles Times; *Hormone Disrupters Cause Sterility*, October 2, 1994

[22] Barna, George; *Trends That are Changing Your Ministry World*, Regal, 1996

[23] Ibid

[24] Hunter, George; *To Spread the Power: Church Growth in the Wesleyan Spirit*, Abingdon, p. 56

[25] Hunter, George; *To Spread the Power: Church Growth in the Wesleyan Spirit*, Abingdon, p. 58

[26] Barna, George; *Trends That are Changing Your Ministry World*, Regal, 1996

[27] Logan, Robert: Clegg, Thomas; *Releasing Your Church's Potential*, ChurchSmart Resources, pp. 4-10

[28] Barna, George; *Trends That are Changing Your Ministry World*, Regal, 1996

[29] London, H.B.; Wiseman, Neil B., *Pastors at Risk*, Victor, p. 120

[30] Logan, Robert; Cole, Neil; *Raising Leaders for the Harvest*, ChurchSmart Resources, pp. 3-1 to 3-28

[31] Allen Roland; *The Spontaneous Expansion of the Church*, Eerdmans, p. 13

[32] Kaiser, Walter C. Jr.; *The Hard Sayings of the Old Testament*, IVP; Bruce, F.F.; *The Hard Sayings of Jesus*, IVP; Brauch, Manfred T.; *The Hard Sayings of Paul*, IVP

[33] Archer, Gleason; *Encyclopedia of Bible Difficulties,* Zondervan

[34] Silvoso, Ed; *That None Should Perish*, Regal, 1994, p.100

[35] Logan, Robert; Clegg, Thomas; *Releasing Your Church's Potential*, ChurchSmart Resources, pp. 4-12